AF560822

POPULATION AND CITIES

By

Dr. M. Lakshmi Narasaiah
M.A., Ph.D.

Professor of Economics,
Co-ordinator, Department of M.B.A. and Commerce,
Special Officer,
Sri Krishnadevaraya University Post-graduate Centre,
Kurnool–518 002
Andhra Pradesh (India)

DISCOVERY PUBLISHING HOUSE
NEW DELHI

First Published-2006
Reprinted-2011

ISBN 81-8356-070-9

Published by
DISCOVERY PUBLISHING HOUSE
4831/24, Ansari Road, Prahlad Street,
Darya Ganj, New Delhi-110002 (India)
Phone: 23279245 • Fax: 91-11-23253475
E-mail:dphtemp@indiatimes.com

Mehra Offset Press
Delhi

Preface

It has been 40 years since India first began breaking runaway population growth. The programmes have largely been failures, including the widely reviled sterilisation campaign of the early '70s that still haunts old men and sends them scurrying at the sight of an unfamiliar face.

By the end of this decade, India's chaotic cities and countless villages are expected to be home for one in every six people on earth.

By early next century, if the projections are correct, more people will live in India than in any other country, including China, Sparse resources will be stretched among even more desperately poor people. Pressure on forests, rivers and agricultural land already under siege will mount.

Growing number of experts in the Third World believe that population control programmes will never work. In China, despite draconian measures to restrict each family to one child, population-control programmes are failing.

Even in Indonesia, touted as one of the world's success stories, the health of thousands of women is jeopardized by contraceptive devices. It is time for hormonal implants in their arms to be removed, but no one has kept track of where they live. There is also evidence many were forced by the military to take part in birth-control programmes.

Although there has been some success in getting women around the world to have fewer children, huge numbers are just now entering their reproductive stage.

The United Nations estimates Six billion by 1998. By the year 2050, those numbers to almost double to 10 billion, and perhaps—if its most optimistic projections are true—level off at 11.6 billion a century later and then begin to fall.

The UN has warned that much depends on action taken during the next decade, saying a delay could mean upto four billion extra people—which was the world's population in 1975—by 2050, and upto 20.7 billion a century later.

But it isn't all bad news. Population growth has slowed in countries where the standard of living has improved and where women have access to education and jobs.

In Thailand, for example, female literacy is now at 90 per cent, and the fertility rate has declined significantly.

If people have jobs, if women can read, the population goes down. It is difficult to tell people, especially in a democracy, what they must do about something as personal as birth control. The rich countries, where population growth is much slower, have become increasingly concerned about the explosion in the Third World.

Dr. M. Lakshmi Narasaiah

Contents

1

Population Growth

Facts and Figures

The World-wide rate of population growth has been essentially the same since 1975, and about 1.7 per cent a year. Fertility is actually going down slightly, from 3.8 in 1975-1980 to 3.3 in 1990-1995. Because of past growth, however, the number of people added each year is still rising. In 1975, the annual addition was about 72 million. In 1992 it was 93 million. It will peak between 1995 and 2000, at about 98 million annually.

Rapid population growth is therefore still the dominant feature of global demographics, and will continue to be so for at least the next 30 years. The 1993 global population of 5.57 billion is projected to increase to 6.25 billion in 2000, 8.5 billion in 2025 and 10 billion in 2050; significant growth will probably continue until about 2150 and a level of about 11.6 billion.

The developing countries proportion of this increase grew from 77 per cent in 1950 to 93 per cent in 1990; between now and the end of the century it will be 95 per cent. Africa and South Asia alone account for 53 per cent.

Asia's population in mid-1993 was 3.3 billion. By 2025, Asia will have 4.9 billion people, equal to the whole of world population in 1986; Africa (700 million) will have 1.6 billion; Latin America (466 million) will have 700 million people.

This overall picture conceals wide variations from country to country and region to region. For example:

- Annual growth 1990-1995 is estimated at 3.0 per cent for Africa, with Asia at 1.9 per cent and Latin America 2.1 per cent. By the large the fastest rates of growth are in the poorest countries.
- The 47 countries officially designated by the demographers as "least developed" accounted for 7 per cent of global increase in 1950, but 13 per cent by 1990.
- Life expectancy has increased by 30 years in East Asia over the last four decades, as against 15 years in Africa, which has 30 of the 47 "least developed" countries.
- Fertility has fallen by 60 per cent in East Asia in the same period, but by only 25 per cent in South Asia and hardly at all in Africa.
- Maternal mortality has been halved in East Asia, but remains virtually unchanged in South Asia and Africa.

Among developing countries, the lowest growth rates are in East Asia and the Caribbean (1.3 per cent). East Asia's growth rates largely reflect the situation in China, which is 85 per cent of the region. Central and South America, South-East and South Asia and Southern Africa lie between 2 and 2.5 per cent; North Africa and West Asia between 2.5 and 3; and the rest of Africa over 3 per cent.

The biggest variation of all has grown up between the industrialised countries of Europe and North America and the rest of the world. In the industrialised countries population growth has slowed or stopped altogether, and fertility is at or below replacement level. Their populations increased by 43 per cent between 1950 and 1990, compared with 162 per cent among the least developed countries and 140 per cent in the other developing countries. This variation will deepen: the populations of Europe and Sub-Saharan Africa, roughly the same in 1985 at about 480 million, will be 500 million and 1500 million respectively by 2025.

Asia has 59 per cent of world population, Latin America 9 per cent and Africa 12 per cent. Africa's share is projected to go up to 19 per cent by 2025, while proportions in the other regions remain about the same. Within Asia the proportions are chaning: China, now 37 per cent of Asia's population, will be 31 per cent by 2025; India will go from 27 per cent to 29 per cent.

2

Population and the Environment
The Global Challenge

As the century begins, natural resources are under increasing pressure, threatening public health and development. Water shortages, soil exhaustion, loss of forests, air and water pollution, and degradation of coastlines afflict many areas. As the world's population grows, improving living standards without destroying the environment is a global challenge.

Most developed economies currently consume resources much faster than they can regenerate. Most developing countries with rapid population growth face the urgent need to improve living standards. As we humans exploit nature to meet present needs, are we destroying resources needed for the future?

Environment Getting Worse

In the past decade in every environmental sector, conditions have either failed to improve, or they are worsening:

Public Health. Unclean water, along with poor sanitation, kills over 12 million people each year, most in developing countries. Air pollution kills nearly 3 million more. Heavy metals and other contaminants also cause widespread health problems.

Food Supply. Will there be enough food to go around? In 64 of 105 developing countries studied by UN Food and

Agricultural Organisation the population has been growing faster than food supplies. Population pressures have degraded some 2 billion hectares of arable land—an area the size of Canada and the US.

Fresh Water. The supply of fresh water is finite, but demand is soaring as population grows and use per capita rises. By 2025, when world population is projected to be 8 billion, 48 countries, containing 3 billion people will face shortages.

Coastlines and Oceans. Half of all coastal ecosystems are pressured by high population densities and urban development. A tide of pollution is rising in the world's seas. Ocean fisheries are being overexploited, and fish catches are down.

Forests. Nearly half of the world's original forest cover has been lost, and each year another 16 million hectares are cut, bulldozed, or burned. Forests provide over US$400 billion to the world economy annually and are vital to maintaining healthy ecosystems. Yet, current demand for forest products may exceed the limit of sustainable consumption by 25 per cent.

Biodiversity. The earth's biological diversity is crucial to the continued vitality of agriculture and medicine—and perhaps even to life on earth itself. Yet human activities are pushing many thousands of plant and animal species into extinction. Two of every three species is estimated to be in decline.

Global Climate Change. The earth's surface is warming due to greenhouse gas emissions, largely from burning fossil fuels. If the global temperature rises as projected, sea levels would rise by several metres, causing widespread flooding. Global warming also could cause droughts and disrupt agriculture.

Toward a Livable Future

How people preserve or abuse the environment could largely determine whether living standards improve or deteriorate. Growing human numbers, urban expansion, and resource exploitation do not bode well for the future. Without practising sustainable development, humanity faces a deteriorating environment and may even invite ecological disaster.

Taking Action. Many steps toward sustainability can be taken today. These include using energy more efficiently; managing cities better; phasing out subsidies that encourage waste; managing water resources and protecting fresh water sources; harvesting forest products rather than destroying forests; preserving arable land and increasing food production through a second Green Revolution; managing coastal zones and ocean fisheries; protecting biodiversity hotspots; and adopting an international convention on climate change.

Stabilising Population. While population growth has slowed, the absolute number of people continues to increase 0 by about 1 billion every 13 years, slowing population growth would help improve living standards and would buy time to protect natural resources. In the long run, to sustain higher living standards world population size must stabilise.

3

Fertility Rates

The Decline is Stalling

During the 1970's, one of the population trends was the reduction in the total fertility rate in several key countries, including the world's two largest nations—China and India. (the fertility rate measures the average number of children born to women in their childbearing years.) In china, the rate dropped precipitously, from 6.4 children per woman in 1968 to 2.2 in 1980. In India, the decline was more modest, but still significant: from 5.8 children per woman between 1966 and 1971 to 4.8 children 1976 and 1981.

These trends helped slow the rate of world population growth from 2.1 per cent between 1965 and 1970 to 1.7 per cent between 1975 and 1980. At that point, however, the decline in the number of children that women were having in these two population giants stalled.

In China, despite the most aggressive and least democratic population control programme in the world, the fertility rate remained around 2.5 throughout much of the 1980s as couples continued to want to marry young and to have two or more children. In India, the overzealous promotion of family planning by the ruling Congress Party through 1977 apparently backfired after the party's defeat and progress toward lower birth rates ran out of steam.

One important lesson from these experiences is that governments must do more than just supply contraceptives; they need to lower the demand for children by making fundamental changes that improve women's lives and increase their access to and control over money, credit, and other resources.

Many countries still register fertility rates above replacement level (See Table), which is generally 2.1 children per woman or basically two children per couple. The total fertility rate for the world as a whole in 1995 was 3.3 ranging from 1.8 in more developed nations to 4.4 in less developed ones (excluding China). In a number of countries, such as Brazil, Egypt, Indonesia, Mexico, and Thailand, fertility rate have been dropping as they did in the 1970s in China and India. At the same time, developing countries have not yet entered the demographic transition.

The demographic transition occurs when both birth rates and death rates in a country drop form historically high levels to low ones that translate into a stable population – one that merely replaces itself with each new generation. Traditionally, although not always, death rates have declined first, following the spread of sanitation and improved health care coverall. Rapid population growth often follows this first phase of the demographic transition, as the gap between fertility and mortality rates widens for a time. Eventually, however, fertility rates fall too.

As the moment, they remain high in a number of countries. The reasons include unequal rights and opportunities for women, as well as inadequate access to birth control. Whatever the reason, the effect is the same: 67 countries, home to 17 per cent of the world population, are at best in the early stages of a transition to low fertility rates. Most of them are in Africa and South Asia, and their populations are likely to double in 20 to 25 years.

This is leading to a two-tiered demographic world that is every bit as worrying as the world of economic haves and have-nots. Countries such as Nigeria and Pakistan are finding it harder to keep up with the demand for food, health care, jobs, housing, and education than countries that are in the middle of the demographic transition.

Population Size, Fertility Rate, and Doubling Time, 20 Largest Countries, 1995

Country	*Fertility Population (millions)*	*Rate (average number of children per woman)*	*Doubling Time (years)*
Italy	58	1.3	3466
Germany	81	1.4	*
Japan	125	1.5	217
United Kingdom	58	1.8	267
France	58	1.8	169
Russia	149	1.7	990
United States	258	2.0	92
China	1178	1.9	60
Thailand	57	2.4	49
Indonesia	188	3.0	42
Brazil	152	3.6	46
Turkey	61	3.6	32
Mexico	90	3.4	13
India	97	3.9	34
Vietnam	72	4.0	31
Philippines	5	4.1	28
Egypt	8	4.6	30
Pakistan	122	6.7	23
Iran	3	6.6	20
Nigeria	5	6.6	23

Source: Population Reference Bureau, 1995 World Population Data Sheet (Washington, DC. 1995).

Even when a country does reach replacement-level fertility, its population can continue growing for decades. There is a built-in momentum created by all the people who have yet to enter their childbearing years. Indeed, the decline in the world's population growth rate stalled in the 1980s in part because even in China, India, and other countries where fertility rates had been dropping, large number of people who had been born in the 1960s reached childbearing age. So even if couples had two or three children instead of five or six, their parents did, the population would grow substantially.

For the world as a whole, even if replacement–level fertility had been achieved in 1990, the population would continue to grow until it reached 8.4 billion in 2150 because of all the young people already alive. This built-in momentum obviously limits how quickly any country can stop population growth. Nevertheless, reaching replacement level fertility is an all-important first step. The 67 countries that have not yet begun the demographic transition—nations in which invariably the government believes fertility levels are to high—could move in the right direction by providing the contraceptive and health care services that would help couples have only the number of children they desire.

4

An Agenda for Change

The world's growing population, combined with unsustainable production and consumption patterns, is putting increasing stress on air, land, water, energy, and other essential resources.

- Development strategies will have to deal with the combination of population growth ecosystem health, technology, and access to resources. Meting the unmet need for family planning and reproductive health services should be part of national sustainable development strategies.
- The world needs to do a better job of forecasting the possible outcome of current human activities, including popualtion trends, per capita resource use, and wealth distribution.

Protecting the Atmosphere. The atmosphere is under increasing pressure from green house gases that threaten to change the climate and from chemicals that reduce the ozone layer. Governments need to:

- Modernize existing power system to gain energy efficiency and develop new and renewable energy sources.
- Promote national energy efficiency and emission standards and develop efficient, cost-effective, and less polluting mass transit systems.

Combating Deforestation. Forests world wide are threatened by uncontrolled degradation and conversion to other uses because of increasing human pressure.

- There is an urgent need to conserve and plant forests in developed and developing countries to maintain or restore the ecological balance and to provide for human needs.
- Governments need to work with business, scientists, local community groups, indigenous people, and the public to create long-term conservation and management policies for every forest region and watershed.

Sustainable Agriculture and Rural Development. Hunger is already a constant threat to over 800 million people, while the world's ability to continue meeting growing demand for food and other agricultural products over the long term is uncertain. Soil erosion, salinisation, water logging, and loss of soil fertility are increasing in all countries.

Agriculture has to meet rising needs mainly by increasing productivity, because most of the world's best croplands are already in use. At the same time further encroachment on land that is only marginally suitable for cultivation must be avoided.

- Sustainable agriculture and rural development will require major adjustments in agricultural, environmental, and economic policies in all countries and at the international level.

Conservation of Biological Diversity. The loss of the world's biological diversity continues, mainly from habitat destruction, over-harvesting, pollution, of foreign plants and animals (known and exotics). This decline in biodiversity is largely caused by human activity and represents a serious threat to our development.

- Develop national strategies to conserve and sustainably use biological diversity and to make these strategies part of overall national development efforts.
- Implement fair sharing of the benefits between providers and consumers of biological resources.
- Protect natural habitats. Promote the rehabilitation of damaged ecosystems.

Protecting and Managing the Oceans. Oceans are under increasing environmental stress from pollution over-fishing, and degradation of coastlines and coral reefs. About 70 per cent of marine pollution comes from sources on land. Countries should commit themselves to control and reduce degradation of the marine environment. They should:

- Build and maintain sewage treatment systems and avoid discharging sewage near shell fisheries, water intakes and bathing areas.
- Develop land-use practices that reduce run-off of soil and wastes to rivers and thus to the seas. Use environmentally less harmful pesticides and fertilisers.
- Control and prevent coastal erosion and silting due to land uses such as unplanned construction.

Protecting and Managing Fresh Water. In many parts of the world there is widespread scarcity, gradual destruction, and increased pollution of fresh water resources. The causes include the inadequately treated sewage and industrial waste, loss of natural water catchment areas, deforestation and other chemicals into the water. The following approaches are key:

- The way to provide all people with potable water and basic sanitation is to adopt the approach "some for all rather than more for some." This approach can be achieved through low-cost services built and maintained at the community level.

- Nations need to identify and protect water resources and see that water is used on a sustainable basis. They need effective water pollution prevention and control programmes. There is a particular need for appropriate sanitation and waste-disposal technologies for low-income, high-density cities.

5

Our Crowded World

It has been 40 years since India first began breaking runaway population growth. The programmes have largely been failures, including the widely reviled sterilisation campaign of the early '70s that still haunts old men and sends them scurrying at the sight of an unfamiliar face.

By the end of this decade, India's chaotic cities and countless villages are expected to be home for one in every six people on earth.

By early next century, if the projections are correct, more people will live in India than in any other country, including China, Sparse resources will be stretched among even more desperately poor people. Pressure on forests, rivers and agricultural land already under siege will mount.

Growing number of experts in the Third World believe that population control programmes will never work. In China, despite draconian measures to restrict each family to one child, population-control programmes are failing.

Even in Indonesia, touted as one of the world's success stories, the health of thousands of women is jeopardized by contraceptive devices. It is time for hormonal implants in their arms to be removed, but on one has kept track of where they live. There is also evidence many were forced by the military to take part in birth-control programmes.

Although there has been some success in getting women around the world to have fewer children, huge numbers are just now entering their reproductive stage.

The United Nations estimates Six billion by 1998. By the year 2050, those numbers to almost double to 10 billion, and perhaps—if its most optimistic projections are true—level off at 11.6 billion a century later and then begin to fall.

The UN has warned that much depends on action taken during the next decade, saying a delay could mean upto four billion extra people—which was the world's population in 1975—by 2050, and upto 20.7 billion a century later.

But it isn't all bad news. Population growth has slowed in countries where the standard of living has improved and where women have access to education and jobs.

In Thailand, for example, female literacy is now at 90 per cent, and the fertility rate has declined significantly.

If people have jobs, if women can read, the population goes down. It is difficult to tell people, especially in a democracy, what they must do about something as personal as birth control. The rich countries, where population growth is much slower, have become increasingly concerned about the explosion in the Third World.

6

Population Growth and Women's Role in India

We have limited economic resources. There is a pressing need to abolish poverty. If population grows unchecked, abolition of poverty becomes very difficult. Due to the rise in population, illiteracy is growing as educational facilities are not expanding as fast as the population. Though employment facilities are being provided, we are not able to solve the unemployment problem. Though production and national income are rising, standard of living is not rising at the same rate. Thus growing population remains a serious drawback.

Conventional wisdom holds that slowing population growth is the key to solving a vast array of social, economic and environmental problems. To be sure, in a world of finite resources, unlimited growth in the number of people requiring food, shelter and work, not to mention access to natural resources, cannot be sustained. But the increasingly singular focus on demographics simply deflects attention from the fundamental social conditions—poverty, inequity, and the abject status of women—of which population growth is not the cause, but the consequence.

In India, as in much of the world, women are last in line for education, job training, credit, and sometimes even food despite the fact that raising the status of women is the most effective way both to reduce birth and to achieve higher standards of health and economic productivity.

In India's tradition-bound society, where childbearing is often the only route to status and security, the majority of women have little to gain from having fewer children. The government, by contrast, is bent on cutting birthrates in half over the next decade, but has shown little commitment to meeting women's needs. And so a vicious cycle is perpetuated. As long as the status of women remains low, voluntary family planning efforts will continue to founder, tempting the government to use pressure to meet its demographic goals.

India will surpass China as the world's most populous country by the middle of the next century. Each day the number of people who lack access to adequate food, healthcare, housing, clean water and education spirals upward.

Female Education

Female education is the single most influential determinant of both lower birthrates and increasing empowerment for women.

Indian society manages to devote fewer resources to educating its girls than its boys. At the household level, cultural restrictions on female behaviour combined with the need for cheap household labour create a sharp gender gap in literacy. In both the Hindu and Moslem traditions, for example, notions of female "modesty" and "purity" dictate that unmarried females remain separate from unrelated males. Because the bulk of India's teachers are men, and most schools educate boys and girls under the same roof, many traditional families keep their daughters home, regardless of their income. Moreover, parents opt to invest in educating girls only when they perceive that long-term gains will outweigh immediate costs.

For the impoverished majority, the expense of sending a girl to school—paying for uniforms, books, and inhibitive especially when young girls are required to work at home and in the fields.

Women's lack of knowledge translates directly into poor nutrition and health for themselves and their offspring. In turn, these conditions causes high infant mortality—for which many women compensate by having more babies.

Nutrition and Health

Nutritional and health status is also marked by gender disparity. Both boys and girls in India are nutritionally disadvantaged, as nearly half of the country's households fail to provide even the minimum daily caloric requirements. But malnutrition is far more prevalent among females than males. From birth, male children consistently receive more and better food than their sisters, even though the nutritional needs of prepubescent boys and girls are virtually identical. Boys, given the same level of illness, are taken to doctors more often than girls. As a result of this neglect, far more girls than boys die in the critical period between infancy and age five.

Discrimination in feeding and healthcare produces one of India's most provocative signs of gender bias: In fact, the ratio of women to men in the country has been declining.

Women and Family Income

Son preference and the subsequently biased allocation of family resources is based on a series of myths the Indian government has failed to combat. One is the notion—not peculiar to India—that female do not contribute to family income. Throughout the world, women bear the "invisible" burden of unpaid domestic work and childbearing, the economic value of which is rarely reflected by official statistics.

Young girls in India generally work longer hours than boys of the same age. By age 10, girls in low income families are working eight or more hours a day assisting their mothers by tending siblings, collecting water and firewood, herding small animals, weeding fields, or facing the daily grind of low-paid child labour in the marketplace.

The poorer the family, the more vital the economic contribution that women and girls make, especially in the growing number of female-headed households.

Indifference Towards Women

The attempts to enhance agricultural productivity disproportionately benefit men.

Expansion of the irrigated area allocated to cash crops, such as groundnut and cotton, has come at the expense of food crops on which women depend to feed their families. And while the mechanisation of ploughing and levelling that comes with these projects reduces the traditional workload of men, that for women actually increases. Women still must carry out by hand the tasks of weeding, turning soil, and harvesting, but over much larger areas.

The result is to deepen women's poverty and enhance the perceived value of having many children to help with chores.

Not surprisingly, the share of married couples of reproductive age using contraceptive—now 40 per cent—is low, and most of these are holder couples who turned to sterilisation (counted as a form of contraceptive) only after having large families.

This bleak situation is shadowed by an ominous fact of history. Past attempts to reduce births in the absence of social changes enhancing women's status have been accompanied by increases in violence against females—in the beating and abandonment of women who don't bear sons, in female infanticide and child neglect, and in the rising use of abortion for sex selection.

Experience shows that even in India, with its immense tangle of troubles, well-designed programmes can produce dramatic improvements in family health while improving women's status and reducing births.

Increasing young girls' access to education and offering older women a chance for learning are essential to increasing female autonomy. Requisite steps include serious efforts to train and hire more female teachers, to set up literacy and tutoring campaigns in every state, and to encourage the growth of women's empowerment groups to foster changes at the village level. These strategies already have been proven in the southern state of Kerala, internationally lauded for its dramatic gains in the health and economic status of women and in slowing population growth.

Equally important are broad public education campaigns to raise awareness of the immense value of women's work and welfare to families and societies. The mass media also could be enlisted in the effort to change dramatically social perceptions of women's roles by depicting positive images of women and their economic contribution to society.

Much of the battle to win recognition of the importance of women's lives and health to societies will have to be fought by women themselves. Indications are that women are responding to the challenge.

By filling the existing demand for quality voluntary family planning services, the government can make cuts in birthrates of at least 25 per cent over the next decade, thereby starting the process towards reducing the country's population. Equally critical to a long term-strategy of sustainable development is a sustained political commitment to improve the status of women throughout India. Only by working towards all these objectives simultaneously can the dreams of women for full partnership in society come true.

7

The Good News About Population Growth

Global population is growing at an ominous pace. Yet new opportunities, if they are seized, along with changes in government policies, could help solve the population problem within two generations. Three facts of the impact of population growth on economic and human development are:

- The countries of the developing world already contain three-quarters of humanity and will soon be home to nine of every 10 people on Earth.
- With but a small fraction of the world's GNP, a tiny percentage of its scientists, the lion's share of its debt and nearly all of its abject poor, these countries have been ill-equipped to absorb the dramatic increases in human numbers that, despite the steadily declining rate of global population growth, has occurred since the end of World War–III.
- Within the next 60 years, between three and seven billion more people will be added to be population of the developing world. Assuming they can sustain such increases, developing countries will double or triple in size before their populations are stabilised a century or more from now. If they cannot, and population size outstrips the resources available to support it, population growth will be slowed faster and sooner, on nature's grim terms.

The conventional wisdom is that because rapid population growth lowers per capita expenditures on education, per capita access to renewable natural resources, and per capita savings rates, it retards economic and social development. But the problem goes beyond this conventional wisdom. There is a lethal synergy that exists in dozens of developing countries between the sheer speed of population growth, on the one hand, and inappropriate government policies that magnify its negative effects, on the other. The former is suggested by the fact that the populations of most developing countries are projected to double in size in 30 years or less. The later is evident in policies that have prevented many developing countries from either slowing such growth or accommodating it gracefully.

It would stretch the capacities of even the most prosperous countries if they had to accommodate the kind of population growth expected in regions including Sub-Saharan Africa and Sough Asia. Without the benefit of prosperity, the indispensable requirement will be for governments to formulate policies that will alleviate rather than exacerbate the economic and social effects of rapid population growth. But as examples from around the developing world illustrate, such policies are in short supply. In Africa, food supplies are inadequate partly because of a pervasive urban bias that leaves farmers with few incentives to produce. In dozens of command economies, housing for low-income families is limited because of anachronistic rent control laws, which have discouraged private developers from building new residential housing units. In other developing countries, significant resources that could be invested in education are diverted for military use. In few of these countries is rapid population growth the main factor retarding economic growth. But in most, such growth has exacerbated the negative effects of short-sighted policies and it will likely do so to a greater degree in the future, for reasons ranging from inexperience in self-government to political opportunism to bureaucratic ineptitude.

High political and institutional barriers thus separate what can be done to mitigate the effects of rapid population growth from what is likely to be done in all to many countries. That's the bad news one has to face as they grapple with the problem of rapid population growth. The good news is that where such barriers have been lowered by far-sighted governments, the results have been hopeful and in some cases dramatic. Sustained high agricultural growth has taken place, in a number of countries—where constraints on small-scale agriculture have been removed. Significant progress has also been achieved by some of the thousands of non-governmental organisation (NGOs) that are playing an increasingly important role in solving population-related problems at the local level in developing countries around the world.

In Bangladesh, meanwhile, the innovative work of two other well-known NGOs – the Grameen Bank and the Bangladesh Rural Advancement Committee – has helped to unleash the productive potential of scores of thousands of poor women, with clear implications not only for economic development but also for fertility reduction. Researchers say the "micro-enterprise" loans given by the banks have changed attitudes towards childbearing by empowering women, raising the "opportunity costs" of having large families and producing a greater degree of parity in marriage relationships. Creating a sense of a future that extends beyond mere day-to-day survival has changed the context for decisions about family size.

Nor is the work of NGOs the only hopeful development weighing in the balance against unprecedented increases in population that are all but certain to occur over the next few decades. As the 21st century approaches there is a heartening convergence of factors that augur well for stabilising global population, sooner perhaps than experts would have thought possible even a decade ago.

The most consequential factor many be the growing desire on the part of men and women around the world for access to family planning services. Millions more, including sexually active young people and couples discouraged from practising family planning by the poor quality of existing services, could be reached by well-run family planning programmes, especially those sensitive to the reproductive health needs of women. Family planning agencies are confident that, in the process of satisfying the existing demand for family planning services, they can create new demand by improving the quality of services and legitimising the small-family model.

Across the institutional spectrum, from national governments in rich poor nations alike, to giant multilateral institutions there is a growing recognition that the future will pose far greater challenges to the human race if rates of population growth are not slowed further. Significantly, that conclusion has recently been endorsed by a growing number of natural scientists who now warn that, without global efforts to slow population growth, science and technology may not be able to redeem the future from want and hunger. One can predict that if current population and consumption trends continue, "science and technology may not be able to prevent either irreversible degradation of the environment or continued poverty for such of the world".

Rates of contraceptive use among men and women, who in every other respect regard themselves as faithful Catholics, are as high as or higher than those of non-Catholics. The lowest birthrates and highest contraceptive use rates on record have been achieved in Catholic World, where abortion is also widely favoured as a back-up in case of contraceptive failure. Similar attitudes are found in the Islamic World, where rapid population growth has prompted theologians to accent a more permissive side of their theology with respect to the use of modern contraceptives. The results have been strong clerical support for family planning programmes.

Beyond the diminished obstacles to progress is the increased opportunity for progress that has been created by the end of the cold war. Freed from the necessity of concentrating on geostrategic threats to peace, policy makers now have the luxury of turning their attention to the global forces that impinge on the peace and prosperity of nations, including the pressure population growth is placing on economic development, food supplies and the natural environment. Worried that such pressures could destabilise the governments of poor nations, prompt interstate conflict over scarce resources, and spur disruptive movements of populations into urban areas or across national frontiers. Western analysts are even now thinking of ways to retool foreign policy to cope with the proliferating number of local threats. One crucial task will be to monitor environmental and economic conditions around the developing world and to provide early warning of regional conflicts. More difficult to implement will be longer-range approaches, including a refashioning of the international trading system to provide more equity to poor nations.

If political leaders are willing and able to capitalise on the opportunity provided by the coming together of this extra-ordinary constellation of circumstances, the population problem could be solved within two generations. If they are not, providing for the welfare of humanity in the century ahead will be more difficult; perhaps, in some of the world's poorest regions, it will prove impossible.

8

Has the Tide Turned?

Successes in Family Planning

Good news from the population front. While during the last decades since 1950 the world population kept growing at an ever faster pace, the yearly increase now seem to be stagnating at around 86 to 90 million. Whereas experts had expected yearly increase of up to 100 million only a short while ago, the actual figures have now turned out to be considerably lower. This means that world population growth may have reached its peak in the 1980s, and that we are now entering a phase of slower growth which, eventually, may lead to a consolidation of world population.

The main reason for the decline in growth rates is the falling fertility of women, especially in developing countries. In Bangladesh, for instance, the number of children per mother has dropped from 6.5 to 3.5 within two decades—a success of family planning which few experts would have thought possible only a few years ago. In spite of all obstacles posed by culture, religion or lacking access to family planning methods, the number of couples practising family planning in developing countries has risen from 14 to 57 per cent during the last 30 years. Even in Sub-Sharan Africa, which still has the highest birth rates of all developing regions, the number of children per woman dropped from 6.7 in 1980 to 6.2 now. Every second woman in Africa says she does not want to have additional children.

The latest figures on population growth will be welc[illegible] who fear that the rapid population increases of the last decades may jeopardize the advances made during the same time in social and economic development. But it is much too early to give the all clear signal. One in four pregnancies is still neither planned nor wanted. And 350 million couples still have no access to modern family planning methods. Powerful traditions in African. Asian and Latin American societies, but also the orthodox views of the Pope and Islamic fundamentalists still stand in the way of effective family planning. No matter how quickly these obstacles will be overcome, world population will rise from its present 5.7 billion to at least 8 billion by the middle of next century. But it makes a big difference whether world population will be at the high or the low end of prognosticated levels—whether there will be 8 or 12 billion people living of the scarce resources and fragile eco-system of our planet.

The Cairo Plan of Action which was adopted at the last World Population Conference focuses on meeting the unmet need in family planning services by the year 2015. Fertility will drop an average of 20 per cent if all women who would like to apply contraception are actually given the physical means to do so. In countries of Africa and South Asia, where contraceptives are still relatively difficult to obtain, the effect of general availability of family planning methods would even be more dramatic.

The key to increasing the use of contraceptives is communication. Information about family planning can be conveyed either through individual communicators in family planning projects of through the mass media. Soap operas on this subject have been very successful in sensitising large parts of the population in Latin America and Asia. Sexual instruction for youths is another important way to spread the knowledge on family planning.

In any case, the current trends are encouraging. Most governments around the world are now convinced that population growth cannot be allowed to go unchecked. The subject of family planning is no longer a taboo. And all those who always say that world conferences like the one in Cairo do not achieve anything should have a good look at the latest figures. Had it not been for the hard and persistent work of UNFPA, IPPF and other organisations the tide may not have turned as quickly as it did. In the Global village in which we all live these days, the word seems to have spread that smaller families are better for the individual and for the world as a whole. More communication on the subject is needed if the present success is to be maintained.

9

Safe Motherhood is a Human Rights Issue

The death of a woman during pregnancy or childbirth is not only an health issue but also a matter of social injustice. Of the human rights currently acknowledged in national constitutions and in regional and international human rights treaties, many can be applied to safe motherhood. Many such treaties and conventions are based on the 1948 Declaration of Human Rights; (1) they include the Convention on the Elimination of All Forms of Discrimination against Women (2) the Convention on the Rights of the Child (3) the European Convention for the Protection of Human Rights and Fundamental Freedom (4) the American Convention on Human Rights (5) and the African Charter on Human and Peoples' Rights (6).

Human rights of relevance to safe motherhood can be grouped into the following four principal categories.

- **Rights relating to life, liberty and security of the person,** which require governments to ensure both access to appropriate health care during pregnancy and childbirth, and women's rights to decide whether, when, and how often to bear children. Governments must therefore address factors within the economic, legal, social, and health systems that deny women these fundamental rights.
- **Rights relating to the foundation of families and of family life,** which require governments to provide access to health-services and other facilities that women

need to establish families and to enjoy life within a family.

- **Rights relating to health care and the benefits of scientific progress, including health information and education,** which require governments to provide access to good sexual and reproductive health care with appropriate referral systems. The measures needed to ensure safe motherhood can be provided through primary health care irrespective of a country's level of economic development. Central to these rights is information on a range of reproductive health issues, including family planning, abortion, and sex education.

- **Rights relating to equality and nondiscrimination,** which require governments to provide access to services such as education and health care without discriminatory grounds such as sex, marital status, age, and socioeconomic class. Discriminatory policies include requirements for a woman to obtain the consent of her husband for particular health care interventions, requirements for parental authorisation which have a differential impact on girls, and laws that criminalise medical procedures that only women need. Governments are in violation of their obligations when they fail to implement laws that effectively protect women's interests or to allocate health resources to meet women's particular need for safe pregnancy and childbirth.

The actions that governments need to take to promote safe motherhood as a human right fall into three groups.

- **Reform of laws** that prevent women from attaining the highest possible levels of health and nutrition needed for safe pregnancy and childbirth and that inhibit access to reproductive health information and services such as laws requiring women in need of health care to seek the authorisation of husbands or other family members first.

- **Implemention of laws** that foster women's rights to good health and nutrition and that protect women's health interests such as laws that prohibit child marriage, female genital mutilation, rape, and sexual abuse. Every effort should be made to implement laws that encourage the healthy timing of births, such as those that support the education of girls, set a minimum age for marriage, and ensure women's access to essential health care.
- **Application of human right** in national legislation and policy to advance safe motherhood.

10

Action for Safe Motherhood

Countries vary enormously in terms of the situations and challenges they face and their capacity to address these. However, experience from around the world over the past decade has demonstrated that a number of features are common to successful efforts to address maternal mortality. Reducing maternal mortality requires coordinated, long-term efforts. Actions are needed within families and communities, in society as a whole, in health systems, and at the level of national legislation and policy. Further, interactions among the interventions in these areas are critical to reducing maternal mortality and to building and supporting momentum for change.

Legislative and Policy Actions

Changes in legislation and policy are essential to ensure safe motherhood. Long-term political commitment is an essential prerequisite. When decision-makers at the highest levels are resolved to address maternal mortality, the resources needed will be mobilised and the essential policy decisions will be taken. Without this level of commitment over the long term, projects cannot become programmes and activities cannot be sustained.

A supportive social, economic, and legislative environment allows women to overcome the various obstacles that limit their access to health care, such as distance from their homes to appropriate health facilities, lack of transport and, more critically, financial and social barriers. Proper maternal health care is limited when women have to pay for services and essential drugs, and when they must bear substantial hidden costs such as time lost for housework, paid employment, food production, and child care. Legislation that supports women's access to care must be formulated to permit health workers at the periphery of the health system to perform specific life-saving functions. Failing this, only highly skilled health professionals, based largely in urban centres, can provide such care, and only women with sufficient money and the means to reach such centres can benefit from it.

With these objectives, careful review of national laws and policies is necessary, particularly in the following areas:

- **Family Planning.** Statutes that restrict women's access to family planning services (e.g. by requiring that a woman be married or that she should have her husband's approval) should be repealed. Policies must ensure that all couples and individuals have access to good-quality, voluntary, client-oriented, and confidential family planning information and to services that offer a wide choice of effective contraceptive methods. Policies should address regulatory, social, economic, and cultural factors that limit women's control over sexuality and reproduction, in order that pregnancies that are too early, too late, or too frequent may be avoided.

- **Adolescents and Children.** Polices and programmes should encourage later marriage and childbearing and an expansion of the economic and educational opportunities for girls and women. Promotion of good nutrition in childhood and adolescence, as well as supplementation if necessary during pregnancy, provides protection for both women and their future children. Policies should also enable adolescents to take responsibility for and protect their sexual and reproductive health, and facilitate their access to health information and services. All children, before they reach the age at which they become sexually active, need to be taught the risks of unprotected sex and help to develop the skills needed to protect themselves from sexual coercion.

- **Barriers to Access.** Assigning health workers trained in midwifery to village-based health facilities can help over-come problems of distance and transport. Health workers should also be trained to deal sympathetically with women patients. Policies should support provision of services at minimum cost, at the same time, health worker should have job security, be paid adequate wages, and be provided with sufficient supplies to do their jobs. Policies that will increase women's decision-making power, particularly in regard to their own health, also essential.

- **Regulation of Practice.** Protocols and statutes aimed at providing both routine maternal care and referral facilities for obstetric complications at each level of the health system need to be developed. Responsibilities at each level for supervision, deployment of health care personnel, remuneration, and reporting procedures must be defined nationally. Development and promotion of education and training curricula are important, as is the setting of national norms and standards to govern the selection of trainees, trainers, and supervisors.

- **Delegation of Authority.** Services should be decentralised so that facilities are available as close to people's homes as possible. Adequate supplies and equipment and trained staff should be available in all health facilities, particularly in rural and remote areas, together with written policies and protocols to guide service provision and to allow certain functions to be delegated to personnel at lower levels (when appropriately trained).

- **Abortion.** Availability of services for management of abortion complications and post-abortion care should be ensured by appropriate legislation. Where abortion is not prohibited by law, facilities for the safe termination of pregnancy should be made available. National policy can discourage unsafe abortion practices by promoting protection against unwanted pregnancy, and national helath campaigns to publicize the risks of unsafe abortion and the need to recognize and seek treatment for abortion complications.

11

Sex and Gender

A World of Difference

Understanding the differences between women and men, and how they are determined, is of key importance in understanding why a gender perspective is so important for development and the elimination of world poverty.

Differences between women and men are determined by biology, on the one hand, and society, on the other.

- Sex marks the distinction between women and men as result of the fundamental biological, physical and genetic differences between them.
- Gender roles are set by convention and other social, economic, political and cultural forces.

The precise boundary between these factors is the subject of fierce debate. Some people believe that the only important difference is that women can bear children and men cannot. Others believe that biology determines a much wider set of characteristics, attributes and capabilities. Whatever the case, the wide variation in the position of women in different societies around the world demonstrates that, unlike sex, gender roles are by no means fixed by nature—they are made by people, and can be renegotiated and changed.

The position of women in society is far from being of academic interest alone. It not only has fundamental consequences for the quality of life of both women and men, but also has a direct impact on a society's prosperity and well-being. The government's policy on international development recognises that gender-based inequality is a major obstacle to the escape from poverty. Studies have shown that developing countries which strive to ensure that women have equal rights have higher rates of economic growth, lower mortality rates, smaller and healthier families, and a better-educated population. Changing gender roles can make a world of difference.

The evidence also shows that gender equality is not luxury which can only be afforded by rich countries. UN data reveals that some developing countries outperform much richer ones in the opportunities they afford women. The better performing countries are scattered throughout the world showing that culture and religion need not be barriers to the advancement of women.

The gender gap in many countries is closing fast. Rapid progress has been made in recent decades. But in no society do women fare as well as men. Women are gaining ground in health and education terms, but still have a long way to go in sharing political and economic opportunities. They continue to suffer high levels of violence and abuse, and in many countries are treated differently to men by the law. These disadvantages are not due to sex differences, but are the result of gender discrimination.

Empowerment, Equality and Equity: What do they Mean?

Women's empowerment, gender equality and equity are key terms in debates about the changes required in the relationships between women and men.

- ***Empowerment*** means individuals acquiring the power to think and act freely, exercise choice, and to fulfil their potential as full and equal members of society.
- ***Equality*** means that women should have the same rights and entitlements as men to human, social,

economic and cultural development, and equal voice in civil and political life. It does not mean that everyone should be the same, or that the benefits of development should be shared in exactly equal proportions by everyone. This would be neither feasible nor desirable, and would not be consistent with the notion of empowerment, which upholds everyone's right to determine their own future and the lifestyle of their choice.

- ***Equity*** means that the exercise of these rights should lead to outcomes which are fair and just, and which enable women to have the same power as men to define and pursue the objectives of development and shape societies of the future.

The difference between equality and equity is important because it underlines the rights of women to define the objectives of development for themselves and to seek outcomes which are not necessarily identical to those sought or enjoyed by men. Women have the right to pursue development paths which reflect their own needs and aspirations.

Upholding these rights is in the interests of men as well as women, because of the wider social and economic benefits brought by gender equality. Because of the universal disadvantages experienced by women, their empowerment is crucial to the achievement of equality and equity, the elimination of poverty and a better world for all.

12

Towards Healthy Cities

More than a third of the urban population in developing world live in housing of such poor quality with such inadequate provision for water, sanitation, drainage, garbage collection and health care that their health is constantly under threat. But, properly planned, cities can be safe and healthy.

In the cities of India, it is common for one child in three to die before the age of five and for virtually all infants, children and adults who survive to have disease burdens many times higher than they should.

Diarrhoea, tuberculosis and respiratory infections (each among the largest causes of death) are generally much increased by over-crowding. Many accidental injuries happen when there are three or more persons living in each small room in shelters made of flammable materials and there is little chance of providing occupants (especially children) with protection from open fires or stoves.

But cities also include some of the India's safest and most healthy neighbourhoods. High densities allow much lower costs for supplying each household with piped, treated water supplies and most forms of health, educational and emergency services.

Sanitation and drainage may be costly in cities, as complex systems are needed to cope with high densities and large population concentrations but city households can generally afford to pay more—and are prepared to do so if they get a good service.

Cities may be considered ecologically unsustainable because of high consumption and waste levels but well planned and managed cities can combine high living standards with remarkably low levels of energy consumption, resource use and wastes. The concentration of people and production creates many more possibilities of collecting and recycling wastes and for walking, bicycling and a high quality public transport.

For many, city-life is one of excessive workloads and drudgery, yet cities remain centres of culture—including the visual and decorative arts, music, dance, theatre and literature. Most cities have a large reserve of young people on whose initiative and energy they could draw to improve condition—yet most such people find that their cities offer them little hope and little prospect of employment. If cities have such potential to provide healthy, stimulating and valued places to live and work for all age groups, why do so achieve this?

Supporting Change

Much of the explanation is the lack of 'good governance'. Good governance in any city means encouragement and support from all levels of government for a great range of investments of capital, expertise and time by individuals, households, communities, voluntary organisations and NGOs—as well as private enterprises. In most cities in India, the total value of investments made by people in their own homes and neighbourhoods exceeds many times the total value of capital investments made by city and municipal authorities. Yet governments and aid agencies usually ignore (or deem illegal) most such efforts.

Most households who want their own home cannot afford to purchase one—or at least one that is legal. They cannot obtain housing loans so the cost of the house purchase can be spread over a number of years—as they cannot meet the (usually) inappropriate conditions set by banks or housing finance institutions. If they turn to building their own home-as most do—they have to occupy or purchase the site illegally. They often have to build on dangerous sites—in floodplains or on slopes with frequent landslides or mudslides—as the cost of safer sites is too high.

Even if they can qualify, for a housing loan; most such loans are for finished houses, not for incremental construction. And even when they have developed their own home and neighbourhood into a viable residential area, governments usually refuse to provide these with roads, water supplies, drains and other essential infrastructure, because they are 'illegal'.

What would cities look like today if governments had supported these individual and community efforts by ensuring that land, building materials, credit and technical advice were as cheap and readily available as possible? Or if government-community partnerships had been formed to, at least, improve water supply, sanitation, drainage and health care.

These work within what is often called the 'social economy'—the great variety of initiatives and actions that are organised and controlled locally and that are not profit-oriented. The social economy includes the work of citizen groups, resident's associations, street or barrio clubs, youth clubs, and parent associations that support local schools. It includes many voluntary groups that provide services for the elderly, the physically disabled or other individuals in need of social. It often includes many initiatives that make cities safer and more fun helping provide supervised play space, sport and recreational opportunities for children and youth. It may provide formal or informal supervision or maintenance of parks, squares, and other public spaces.

The social economy not only 'gets things done' but also creates a dense fabric of relationships that allows citizens to work together in identifying and acting on local problems.

Its value to a 'healthy city' is enormous, even if it is often forgotten by governments and international agencies.

The capacity of city authorities to govern is not the same as the capacity to invest, since these authorities can do much to encourage and support the social economy. City authorities can often greatly increase the supply and reduce the cost of land for housing by changing inappropriate regulations, streamlining planning and land use control, procedure and making better use of publicly owned land.

City authorities should also have the main role in enforcing legislation on, air and water pollution and occupational health and safety. This does not require large investments by public authorities, but it can do much to improve health and the quality of life in a city. Good governance also means managing competing claims and finding common ground between enterprises, trade unions and residents about what should be done to make the city more healthy.

Achieving a healthy city needs a representative political system through which the priorities of citizens and businesses can influence policies and actions. Democratic structures remain among the best checks on the misallocation of resources by city and municipal governments. Actively involving a wide range of local groups in developing 'city governance' helps ensure that the different priorities of a wide range of groups are addressed.

The key issue is not so much identifying what should be done to achieve more healthy cities. This is well known. It is identifying how it should be done, especially how governments and international agencies can support a vast range of activities by individuals, households and communities that help build and maintain healthy cities—which to date they have ignored or even (for many governments) repressed.

13

Sustainable Cities

Today almost one half of the world's population lives in cities. The world's cities are growing by one million people each week. Cities today play a significant role in development. They continue to attract migrants from rural areas because they enable people to advance socially and economically. Cities offer significant economies of scale in the provision of jobs, housing and services, and are important centres of productivity and social development.

However, the stress of this rapid urban population growth is often overwhelming. The long list of afflictions includes urban poverty rates of up to 60 per cent. Despite growing investments, more than one third of the urban population live in substandard housing. Forty per cent of urban dwellers do not have access to safe drinking water or adequate sanitation. Primarily due to a rapid growth and a deteriorating urban environment, at least 600 million people in human settlements (cities, towns and villages) already live in health-and life-threatening situations, and almost 50 per cent of these are children.

The high rate of urban population growth in most regions has led to common problems: congestion, lack of funds to provide basic services, a shortage of adequate housing and declining infrastructure, to name a few.

While these problems are occurring in urban areas, cities still have an important role to play in protecting the global environment in the face of rapid urban population growth. Agricultural and livestock production in rural areas are pushing farther and farther into ecologically fragile regions and cannot support growing population. The finite land and water resources make it imperative that human settlements be carefully planned. Indeed, sustainable urbanisation will ease the pressures caused by encroachment on fragile natural habitats.

India's cities offer a bewildering sight to any visitor: the congestion caused by rapid population growth and a continuing rural-urban drift often leads to conditions which defy all rules of orders, hygiene and environmental safety. Inadequate leadership, corruption and mismanagement have a harmful effect on the physical, environmental, social and ethical structures of cities in India.

Millions of people live in inadequate conditions—without piped water, electricity, security of land tenure, access to roads or health facilities. The means available for production and financing of housing and urban infrastructure are too limited to meet basic needs.

Reducing Poverty and Creating Jobs

Urban poverty is rising at an alarming pace, especially among women. The informal economic sector—which makes a substantial contribution to the delivery of services, production of goods, building of infrastructure and housing construction—often provides the only opportunity for the urban poor to make a living.

Local informal housing construction, for example, generates up to 20 per cent more jobs than high-cost construction. Street hawking, waste recycling and food production are primary sources of income among the urban poor and are illustrative of the creativity of survival strategies.

However, the informal sector itself is often highly exploitative and fails to raise people's economic development beyond mere subsistence. Larger economic strategies and more participatory urban planning approaches that take stock of local skills, technologies and materials are required to generate new and better-paying job opportunities in cities and towns.

Incorporating Environmental Concerns

In 1992 the Rio Conference on Environment and Development designed the Agenda 21 Programme of Action to help save a planet endangered by environmental neglect and plagued by poverty and underdevelopment. Most of the goals agreed to in Rio can become reality only through local action in cities where environmental threats are increasing. Again, it is the urban poor who are particularly endangered by environmental degradation and pollution. The world's Agenda 21 will fail if the city's environmental agenda (population, inadequate sanitation, water supply and waste management) is not addressed. This is being recognised by local authorities all over the world.

Sustainable development in the twenty first century will to a large degree, depend upon how cities, towns and villages everywhere interact with the environment and utilise natural resources.

Increasing Awareness of Gender Issues

Women and men use and experience cities differently, according to their roles, responsibilities and access to resources. For example, when basic services are lacking in a settlement, more often than not it is women who take on responsibilities such as water collection and refuse disposal. Women often have unequal access to resources such as property, credit, training and technology. All of these factors must be addressed urgently, as they make it harder for women to improve their living standards and those of their children.

Disaster Mitigation Relief and Reconstruction

As cities become large and more densely populated, they become increasingly vulnerable to natural and man-made disasters such as earthquake, floods, industrial hazards, epidemics, civil strife and wars. Poor people are forced to live in the most exposed, dangerous and cramped conditions; in flood-prone areas, on steep hillsides or near polluted streams and waste dumps. As a result, they are most likely to lose their homes or their lives when disasters occur. Better planning, access to affordable urban land, and improved construction methods can reduce the extent of catastrophes.

These successful and sustainable approaches to poverty eradication; managing the urban environment; providing access to land, shelter and finance; empowering women and men; and many other issues will have to be documented and disseminated widely.

14

Cities Residents to the Rescue

In the next ten years, the number of people living in cities will rise to around 3.3 billion. Tokyo already has a population of 27 million, Sao Paulo (Brazil) 16.4 million, and Bombay 15 million. World Bank forecasts show as much as 80 per cent of the developing countries, economic growth occurring in the cities and major conurbations.

There are both positive and negative aspects to these developments. At each stage in the history of urbanisation, environmental conditions in cities were improved dramatically. The process was often slow, but over time, many epidemic diseases have been controlled, the supply of clean water and the removal of wastes have become routine, the risks of fire have been contained, and standards of comfort and cleanliness have risen to unprecedented levels. Cities could not have become as large and as numerous as they are now if environmental conditions had remained unchanged.

In a curious way, the pollution that cities suffer is largely due to their wealth. The rich consume a great deal more energy, water, building materials and other goods than the poor, and thus produce much more waste. This is what is happening; in the cities where rapid industrialisation is taking place—only the rich enjoy the benefits of piped water and refuse collection.

Increasingly Insanitary Conditions

There is another, often tragic, aspect to this situation. The poorest of the poor are reduced to living in outer-edge shantytowns in extremely insanitary conditions and, lacking the resources to deal with the problem, the city as a whole has to endure congestion and air and water pollution. Some towns and cities are expanding at a rate of over 7 per cent a year, municipal sanitation departments are no longer able to cope, and it is estimated that as many 30 per cent of the population are without running water.

In many of the world's major cities runaway population growth, an epidemic of Aids and rising social tensions have been combined in the last few years with a steep drop in incomes. The population living on the outer edges of the cities continues to grow apace, hundreds of thousands of people are without running water and 15 per cent of them without sanitation of any sort. Various voluntary bodies and non-governmental organisations have got together, often successfully.

Water and the Environmental, Crisis

One key problem concerns the availability of clean water. Some progress has been achieved as a result of the International Drinking Water Supply and Sanitation Decade, but in 1994 at least 220 million people still lacked a source of drinking water near their homes. In some cases, communities of 500 or more inhabilitants are served by a single tap. In some towns, communal taps function for only a few hours a day, so that people cannot build up sufficient reserves of water for their personal needs if it takes too long to fetch or if the water to be carried long distance.

As there are no proper sanitation measures, the disadvantaged members of the population have to drink dirty water, fish in polluted stream, and eat vegetables that have been grown by the side of refuse tips.

A further major problem arises from the threefold harmful impact of cities on the environment; urban development on agricultural land, the extraction and exhaustion of natural resources, and the dumping of refuse.

Growing pressure on coastal regions, where nearly a billion people now live, is doing serious damage to the marine environment. Development activities pose a threat to nearly half the world's coasts.

Towns originally offered people a place of refuge, of mutual help and culture. According to nineteenth-century town-planning theorists, they should supply all human needs. They were supposed to be the very stuff of civilisation. That was not to be, and therefore whenever the authorities throw their hands, dismayed by the scale of the problems and lacking the political will, money or resources to cope with them, personal initiatives are those most likely to succeed.

15

In Defence of the City Urban Development a Key for Survival

The figures sound alarming. The towns and cities in developing countries are growing faster than ever before. By the year 2000, 2.2 billion people will live in the cities of the Third World. Their numbers are expected to double by the year 2025. But many of the cities in Africa, Asia and Latin America are already bursting at the seams. Some of the so-called megacities have more than 10 or 15 million inhabitants. Many of them live in unplanned squatter settlements, without water and electricity, in an environment of squalor, poverty, crime and disease. Nevertheless, the cities seem to have lost nothing of their attraction for the rural populations. Although the larger share of the population increase in the cities of developing countries is caused by the children of people already living there, the rural-urban migration continues unabated. The cities still offer better chances for employment and education, they provide a better physical infrastructure, better health facilities and a more interesting life. Miserable as conditions in the cities often appear to be, they are usually much better than those in the rural areas. It is, therefore, an illusion to believe that the growth of the cities could be checked by concentrating the development efforts on the countryside. There is no alternative to urban development in a world will soon count some 8 billion people.

Cities have always been in the vanguard of development. The ancient civilisations of Mesopotamia,

Egypt, Greece and Rome were city cultures which for the first time in human development created large, well-governed states. In Europe during the Middle Ages, the creation of towns and cities offered the rural populations a chance to evade the oppression by feudal authorities and become free citizens. Local self-government in medieval towns is at the cradle of democratic development. There is a clear separation of competence between the national, state and local level of government leaving citizens an opportunity to decide on matters which directly affect their own local environment. It is worth looking at this model when discussing ways organised to improve city governance and allow for more participation of the population.

Another fact worth looking at is the size of cities in Industrialised countries. Although about three-quarters of the people live in urban areas, there are only a handful of really big cities.

Of course, the growth of towns and cities in developed countries is the result of a long historical process, deeply rooted in the particular political and economic conditions of the past centuries. In developing countries today, other conditions prevail which favour the emergence of ever bigger urban conglomerations. However, governments are able, thorough appropriate investment and the location of industries educational facilities, or housing policies to influence the settlement trends in their respective countries in favour of smaller cities.

One point seems certain, though, when considering the pros and cons of city development: the severe environmental problems facing mankind today can only be solved if people live in highly concentrated settlements rather than being spread out evenly over the whole countryside. Environment-friendly mass transport, for instance, is only possible in the cities. Fossil fuel consumption which adds to the pollution of the atmosphere will be lower when people live close to their places of work. Their supply with food, water, electricity and social amenities is cheaper and uses up fewer resources when distances are short. The use of land for housing, transport, and industry is less when buildings grow in height rather than space. Even refuse disposal and wastewater management is easier to organize in a big city than in the countryside.

What is important then is not to question the validity of city development, but to make cities and towns a better place to live in. Good city governance, more involvement of the population in decision-making, more attention paid to environmental hazards caused by congestion and low safety standards are some of the demands that must be met to cope with the problems of the cities. There is no reason to bedevil the city as the most successful form of human settlement. Since the times of Babylon, it has also been a place where many different peoples and cultures meet. A generation from now, half the human population will live in cities. We should see this as a chance for human survival.

16

Urbanisation in India and Limitations

Urban growth is an undeniable fact of the future in India. Only 1 in 10 people lived in cities when this century began; nearly half will by century's end. Urban migration accounts for a large share of this rapid growth. Upto 60 per cent of the people in many cities in India live in burgeoning, impoverished squatter settlements.

Allowing urban development to spread out upon undisturbed land exacerbates automobile dependence and destroys the natural environment. Yet it is impossible to truly halt development; prohibiting growth in one jurisdiction merely shifts it to neighbouring areas, The key to a livable and viable future for the India's urban areas is neither to encourage sprawled growth nor to try to stifle growth altogether—but rather, to encourage compact growth.

Forward-looking Municipalities have discovered that compact development can accommodate expanding populations without despoiling the surrounding environment. These cities are actually using urban growth to their advantage: for example, compact development, by making public transit, cycling, and walking more practical, reduces reliance on cars so that less energy is used and less pollution generated. Filling in their under-used space has allowed these cities to become more pleasant and convenient places to live. With less space paved over for parking lots and urban highways, more room is available for homes, workplaces, and green space.

In the long run, population stabilisation—via more effective family planning and elimination of poverty—is essential to the future of the Indian cities. But it will take decades to stabilise population growth. In the mean-time it is essential for urban areas to begin redesigning themselves. With compact development, urban areas can meet people's expanding needs by making the most of existing space.

Somewhere to Grow

Many cities have so much underused space that they could develop for decades to come without bulldozoing another square yard of undisturbed land. Although much underuse of property results from individuals and companies holding it for speculation, local governments themselves frequently hold large amounts of vacant real estate. Surplus government buildings, and other public holdings often stay idle while growth mushrooms at the city's edge. In India great potential for filling in underused space lies in redistributing urban land ownership. Land reform, granted, is among the most difficult political moves a government can undertake, Yet the need for such an effort is difficult to deny.

Cities have tremendous scope for making urban growth more compact by establishing urban growth boundaries outside of which further development is prohibited. Greenbelts surrounding cities perform this function in India. Cities of strict land-use planning charge that urban growth boundaries and other bold measures encroach on individual freedoms. Yet guiding development more rationally can in fact do more to protect people's rights, while keeping cities livable.

Urban Density: The Real Story

Often, people move out to the suburbs seeking open space and bonds with nature that come only in a rural setting. Yet most of these residents continue to maintain an urban life style—commuting to jobs in the city and demanding an assortment of urban amenities found in suburban shopping malls. The result is neither urban nor rural living, but a destructive compromise that the environment cannot sustain.

The low-density suburban model not only has come at a high ecological price, but it also has failed to deliver on many of its promises. Seeking freedom, mobility, fresh air, and access to open space, many suburbanites instead encounter long commutes and traffic jams caused by the dispersed communities' nearly exclusive reliance on private automobiles. Suburban life promises escape from crime in the city, only to trade that danger for the far greater chance of being injured or killed in a car accident. And a new form of social inequity has emerged, stranding anyone who cannot drive or afford a car.

Although denser land use could help solve the environmental, social, and aesthetic problems of sprawl, widespread misconceptions about increased density—even moderate density—often prevent communities from adopting compact land use strategies. Contrary to popular belief, augmenting the density of development does not create a harsh physical environment. Planners and citizens, often assume that moderate and high-density land use are synonymous with crime, poverty, and squalor. Yet there is no scientific evidence to support a direct link between these social problems and density.

Transport's Missing Link

One of the most destructive by products of low-density sprawl is an automobile-dependent transport system. The pattern of urban development dictates whether people can walk or cycle to work or whether they need to travel dozens of miles; it also determines whether a new bus or rail line can attract enough riders. Despite this obvious link, city layouts often are too dispersed to foster efficient transportation. Many of the India's cities have failed to implement compact land use as a transport strategy; few foresaw that an automobile orientation would later plague them with traffic jams, deadly accidents, harmful noise, and smog, while marginalising people who do not own cars. A more rational approach for Indian cities would be to integrate homes not only with workplaces but with commercial, recreational, and other land uses so they are easily accessible without cars. Such reforms ideally would not hamper developers or impose uniformity, but instead would lift restrictions that create unnaturally one-dimensional districts.

The key to making integrated zoning work well as a transport strategy is to encourage urban development that is dense enough to promote alternatives to cars. For example, transport planners estimate that an Indian city typically requires at least seven dwellings per acre in a given area to support reasonably frequent local bus service, nine dwellings for light rail, and 15 dwellings for an express bus. These moderate densities can be reached by mingling clusters of single-family homes with garden apartments and two-to six-storey apartment buildings.

Many large cities are finding that the most transport-efficient land use pattern combines a compact, well-mixed downtown with several outlying, high-density areas—all linked by an extensive public transport system. This way, people can walk, cycle, and take short public transport trips within a given area and reach other areas via express bus or rapid light rail.

Room Enough for All

Attempts to slow or stop growth shut out many groups of people—any by restricting the supply of housing, tend to inflate home prices. Compact growth, by contrast, can help create diverse communities and promote smaller, more affordable housing.

Cities of India can combine compact growth with strategies to increase the supply of land available for low and moderate-income homes. India can made use of measures to prevent speculation, a process whereby land-owners in nearly all free-market societies hold land as an investment for future wind-fall gains, rather than putting it to current use. Speculation puts upward pressure on real estate prices and idles great amounts of urban land.

By taxing vacant land according to its true worth in the market, cities can make these parcels less attractive as an investment vehicle. Local governments typically assess such properties at far less than their market value, effectively rewarding property owners for keeping their land idle. More accurate property assessment encourages redevelopment. Cities can go a step further to tax vacant land more heavily than developed parcels. To avoid spurts of sprawled growth, however, it is critically important to combine these tax strategies with clearly defined growth frontiers—such as greenbelts and urban growth boundaries—that contain development within the existing urban area.

Municipalities can enhance the supply of affordable housing require each house to occupy its own spacious lot with controls that promote a variety of housing types, including smaller and multi-family homes.

A more immediate remedy to the housing crunch felt in many cities, where homes tend to be large, is to allow single-family home owners to rent out small apartments within their homes. The size of the average household is shrinking steadily as couples have fewer children and more people choose living arrangements other than the nuclear family. As a result, many homes built for larger households can create an extra unit in a converted basement, garage, attic, or even an added story.

Laying the Groundwork

Creating compact cities requires a commitment by planning authorities and governments at the local, regional and national levels. Adequate local planning institutions are especially lacking in the developing world. Municipal government in India often have neither the authority to guide land use nor the funds to provide basic services. With few exceptions, urban planning is a relatively recent phenomenon in India.

Compact growth of cities also hinges on regional cooperation, an important tool for handling conflicts between the interests of individual localities and those of the broader region. All cities in India are required to plan their own development according to stipulated goals, such as energy conservation, protection of open space, and provision of affordable housing. These statewide planning requirements not only enhance regional cooperation, but they also give cities the backing they need to apply a comprehensive, long-term vision to their land use planning.

Finally, the effectiveness of urban planning can be fully achieved only if governments remove the conflicting incentives posed by other national policies. Among the greatest barriers to compact urban development are artificially low petrol prices, which encourage dependence on cars.

If the barriers to efficient land use were removed, what would a compact city look like? Much of the vast space normally devoted to automobile parking in a sprawled, car-dependent city would be planted in trees and flowers, or used for building homes. Old properties would be received for new uses; a 19th-century warehouse into apartments, a vacant lot into a public park, for instance, the downtown area would be lived in day and night, with apartments and offices occupying the floors above ground-level shops. Each district would be home to a variety of jobs, shops, and day care centres, all within an easy walk or bicycle ride. People could travel quickly to other parts of the city and outlying areas via rapid rail and express bus lines.

On a rapidly urbanising India, societies can take greater command of their fate by more consciously determining the use of urban land. Whether surrounded by affluent suburbs or makeshift shantytowns, the cities can protect the environment and better address the needs of current and future generations by planning for compact growth.

17

City Politics
A Voice for the Poor

By 2020 the world's urban population will rise by almost 1.5 billion. Cities and towns house a growing proportion of poor people, partly because of the increased share of urban population of the total but also because economic recession and adjustment policies often hit poorer urban residents the hardest. Cities are associated with economic growth and wealth generation and yet inequality is high. Poor people generally live in substandard conditions, may not benefit from job creation, and suffer high levels of pollution, crime and violence.

How can city governments cope with the challenges of population growth and increased global economic competition, and meet the needs of poor residents/is urban governance responsive to the needs of the poor? Are the agencies responsible for city government, especially the municipalities, addressing poor people's needs? Are NGOs and people's organisations playing a greater role in service delivery? Or is their role one of advocacy and lobbying? If so, how do they relate to the formal political system? Can governments fulfil their responsibilities, including poverty reduction? How can the well-being of poor urban governance institutions priorities their needs? In assessing the responsiveness of city government to poor people, three key questions are addressed:

How can the Poor Influence the Agenda of the Institutions of Urban Governance?

The influence of poor residents on decision-making is controlled, in part, by the formal political system. Democratisation gives people a vote. However, this vote means more when elected representative depend on the political support of poor people—where they are a majority, or are well organised, or where there is a ward-based system. If poor people are organised enough, to articulate their needs and demand a fair share of urban resources. NGOs can help poor groups organise better and provide support for networking.

Where poor people are not organised it does not mean they are politically powerless. Poor people in this situation, however, are prey to the disadvantages of patronage and unlikely to be included in formal consultative processes. For an electoral system to be truly responsive, specific mechanisms and channels, such as consultative and participatory processes at city and sub-city levels, are needed to complement representative democracy. Athough, these channels do not necessarily include the poorest or make a marked difference to resource allocation, pro-poor decisions are unlikely without them.

How can Cities Finance their Activities and Reduce Poverty?

Democratisation has not, in many countries brought allocation of financial resources or the revenue-raising capacity for local governments to fulfil their responsibilities. The responsiveness of city governments to poor people's needs thus depends, on whose voices are heard in the arenas of political decision-making. Responsiveness also depends on how available financial resources are allocated and how the programmes they finance are designed. There is scope, for city governments to increase property and business revenues, and to borrow for capital investment. Whether increased financial resources benefit poor people depends on how the demands of external investors and creditors are reconciled with the demands of poor residents; the willingness of politicians and officials to address the distributive implications of existing and planned spending; and efficient transparent financial management. If funds are made available to sub-city levels of government or if expenditure can be influenced by ward councillors, the funds might then be used to meet the priorities of poor residents.

What are the Necessities of Urban Living and how can Access to them be Ensured?

An Adequate Income: Work opportunities should be the top priority. City governments can, however, support the urban economy in general and the economic activities of the poor in particular. Firstly they can ensure that the basic services are efficiently provided. Secondly city governments can refrain from activities that destroy the assets and livelihoods of the poor, especially eviction of informal settlements and micro-enterprises. Savings and credit schemes can be more appropriately organised at a community level and supported by NGOs.

Land Ownership is a common aspiration for poor households. A home with secure tenure (not necessarily title) provides security, an appreciating asset, access to services, and a base for economic activities. Increasing the opportunities for poor households to gain access to a well-located plot of land is an important component of any poverty reduction strategy. Many never fulfil their dream and the needs of those who cannot, or do not wish to become home owners should not be neglected, however.

Local government is potentially more responsive to poor residents than are central government agencies, although this depends on the balance of political power and bureaucratic perceptions. The limited ability of the public sector to secure benefits for the poor from public-private partnerships in land development, suggest that more informal arrangements and the involvement of CSOs may be better ways forward.

Environmental Services: Land alone will not reduce poverty but must be linked to a healthy living environment—a package of appropriate and affordable environmental services, such as public transport, water and sanitation, solid waste collection, and energy for cooking and lighting. Rather than discussing appropriate standards, detailed issues of financing and affordability or how continued provision can be assured for each of these services, the research focused on how far decision making channels mechanisms and partnership arrangements ensure that providers are responsive to the needs and priorities of poor residents.

Collaborative planning and decision-making arrangements are one promising alternative, despite the current shortcomings of participatory budgeting. For responsiveness to the poor to be built in to such processes, local bureaucrats need to change their attitudes and working practices. Is it possible and acceptable for poor people to have to rely on their own resources their households and networks—resources that are very limited? Informal networks and links can, however, provide mutual support and access to politicians and bureaucrats, community associations though not always present, inclusive or transparent, can play an important role in articulating poor residents views and in organising self-help activities. There is scope for formal representative community organisations, for informal links between peoples' organsiations and the power structures, and for networking between people's groups. NGOs can play an important role in developing the capacity of community organisations and in facilitating networking. Where NGOs play a role in service delivery. However, there is a danger that the resulting close relationship with local government detracts from their ability to empower poor people and challenge inappropriate policies. City governments, it is clear, cannot cope with the challenges of population and economic growth and respond to the needs of poor people alone. Only in alliance with other actors is there some hope that poverty can be overcome. For CSOs, many of which were forged during struggles for democratisation, this implies moving beyond confrontation to engagement. To form alliances between CSOs and city governments that put the interests of the poor first, poor people must be able to exercise their political rights.

18

Cities at the Forefront

The rapid growth of cities in the developing world puts them in the forefront of the struggle for improved living standards and protection of the environment. Since 1950 the urban population has more than tripled, from just over 750 million to about 3 billion. By 2030 some 5 billion people will live in cities. In the developing world the urban population is projected to double from 1.9 billion in 2000 to be just under 4 billion by 2030.

Worldwide, about three fourths of all current population growth is urban. Cities are gaining an estimated 55 million people per year—over 1 million new residents every week from in-migration and natural population increase within cities. In developing countries many cities are growing two or three times faster than population growth for the country as a whole. As cities grow ever larger, their impact on the environment grows exponentially.

The Rise of Megacities

The UN coined the term megacities in 1970s to describe cities with 10 million or more residents. As recently as 1975 there were only five megacities worldwide. Currently, there are 19 megacities, of which 15 are in developing countries. By 2015 the number of megacities will grow to 23 which is explained in Table 3.1. Megacities have captured public interest because cities this large are unprecedented in history and because of the popular perception that human well-being will decline in such dense concentration of people.

Millions of people move from the countryside to the city to seek a better life, but they often find that their lives become more difficult. In many cities 25 per cent to 30 per cent of the urban population live in poor shanty towns or squatter settlements, or they live on the streets. Of Rio de Janerio's 10.6 million resident, for example, 4 million live in squatter settlements and shanty towns, some perched precariously on step hillsides. Nevertheless cities, in developing countries continue to attract more and more people.

Table 18.1: Megacities of the World

Cities with 10 Million or More Inhabitants, 1975, 2000 and 2015 (Population in Million)

City-1975	Population	City-2000	Population	City-2015	Population
Tokyo	19.8	Tokyo	26.4	Tokyo	26.4
New York	15.9	Mexico City	18.1	Bombay	26.1
Shanghai	11.4	Bombay	18.1	Lagos	23.2
Mexico City	11.2	Sao Paulo	17.8	Dhaka	21.1
Sao Paulo	10.0	Shanghai	17.0	Sao Paulo	20.4
		New York	16.6	Karachi	19.2
		Lagos	13.4	Mexio city	19.2
		Los Angeles	13.1	Shanghai	19.1
		Calcutta	12.9	New York	17.4
		Buenos Aires	12.6	Jakarta	17.3
		Dhaka	12.3	Calcutta	17.3
		Karachi	11.8	Delhi	16.8
		Delhi	11.7	Metro Manila	14.8
		Jakarta	11.0	Los Angeles	14.1
		Osaka	11.0	Buenos Aires	14.1
		Metro Manila	10.9	Cairo	13.8
		Beijing	10.8	Istanbul	12.5
		Rio de Janerio	10.6	Beijing	12.3
		Cairo	10.6	Rio de Janerio	11.9
				Osaka	11.0
				Tianjin	10.7
				Hyderabad	10.5
				Bangkok	10.1

Source: UN Population Division, March 2000 (p: 239).

Cities occupy only 2 per cent of the world's land surface, but city populations have a disproportionate impact on the environment. For example, London requires rough 60 times its land area to supply its 9 million residents with food and forest products. Because commerce and trade have spread dramtically in recent years, city resident consume resources not just from surrounding areas, but, increasingly, from around the world. Urban areas also export their wastes and pollutants, affecting environmental and health conditions far from the cities themselves.

What can be done?

In the long run, slowing population growth would help ease the pressure on cities, buying time to make improvements in technology. Municipalities also can take a number of steps now—building better transportation systems, promoting recycling, and encouraging water conservation.

Public Transportation: One of the best investments that cities can make – both environmental and economic is an efficient mass transportation system. In many cities people waste great amounts of time and fuel going nowhere because traffic congestion is servere. In many urban areas vehicular exhausts account for 50 per cent to 70 per cent of polluting emissions, curbing the number of motor vehicles by offering transportation alternatives would save energy and reduce pollution. Some cities for example, Amsterdam and Copenhagen—have helped ease the transportation crisis by creating special traffic lanes for bicycles and by urging bicycle use.

Recycling: Recycling mountains of urban waste into new resources makes sense both environmentally and economically. Recycling saves natural resources and reduces the amount of trash deposited in landfills or dumped into rivers, lakes, and the ocean. Also, for every million tons of solid waste, about 1,600 recycling jobs could be created in developed and developing countries alike.

Water Conservation: Urbanisation dramatically increases per capita freshwater use, as millions of households gain access to piped water, as industry increases, and as large-scale irrigated agriculture replaces subsistence farming. Cities everywhere need to adopt water conservation measures.

19

Urbanisation and Globalisation

How we handle globalisation will determine whether our cities and our civilisation will be divided and violent or user-friendly and peaceful. We cannot get a clear picture of urban life in the 21st century, especially in the poor countries of the South, unless we take into account the phenomenon of globalisation, which has already brought dramatic changes make their first appearance. So it is there too that the great upheavals of the next century will take place.

Globalisation gives shape to the "Global Village". The "information era" that it ushers in compresses time and we are now living in a world speeded up as never before. Worldwide urbanisation is proceeding at a similar rate and its pace in the poor countries of the South seems terrifying. By 2025, two-thirds of humanity will be living in cities and towns, where the best opportunities in life tend to be.

Globalisation also accentuates a "new urban geography" in both North and South. Islands of rich consumers are springing up in cities amid an ocean of deprived people. More and more unemployed people, immigrants, minorities and the homeless, are pushed into cities by pressure from "market economies". As a result, all urban areas—not just those in the poor countries of the South—will have to deal with growing internal tensions. In New York, for example, the poorest 20 per cent of the population earns 15 times less than the richest 20 per cent.

Cities have always had their smart neighbourhoods and their dangerous areas. But such social and geographical segregation has changed in pace and scale because of the growth in the urban population, the increase in "illegal" migrants and rising uncertainty.

In fact, we have entered a period of historical transition, where discontinuities prevail over adjustment. Radical changes in the nature of production and jobs and the incredible concentration of capital in the hands of the financial sector and speculators weigh much heavier in our lives these days than the state's efforts to adjust and improve the market economy. Segregation in cities has been given a new lease of life whose consequences we do not know. It has reached unprecedented dimensions because of the explosive growth of urban areas.

According to one scenario, things will go badly. The growing pace of globalisation will increase uncertainty about the future. Fear and defence mechanisms will grow among people and institutions, fuelling intolerance, xenophobia and mistrust of everything new or foreign. Urban tensions will manifest themselves with increasing violence, and segregation will sharpen. Public areas will be abandoned and become dangerous no-man's lands, the wretched abode of society's rejects. Cities will lose their original function of being a crossroads for meeting and exchange.

If globalisation also continues to go hand in hand with deregulation of financial markets and an unchanged level of indebtedness of poor countries, the latter will not be able to maintain their urban infrastructures. And if on top of this there is corruption and lack of political will, challenges to the system will increase and violence will grow. Cash-strapped authorities will respond with undemocratic mafias which provide them with funds.

According to a second scenario, everything will be all right. In line with the principle that "everything the state does is public, but the state doesn't control everything that is public," a new social contract will be drawn up between the state, the market, the working population and civil society, including NGOs. Cities will develop a new quality of life by providing citizens with forum for exchange. Jobs will be created in the social sector, in the fields of the environment, education, research, culture and leisure, opening up possibilities for young people.

In the countries of the South, long-term development strategies will be drafted and urban planning practiced, taking advantage of the opportunities provided by globalisation but without falling into its traps. Town planning will become part of the political process, and the state will work with the private sector, monitored by institution of civil society. Adequate housing will be built with the help of micro-credit and controls on the price of building material. Improved infrastructures will enable marginal areas to become part of the civilised part of the city. Democracy will come up with new ways of governing with the help of networks of involved citizens.

In a transitional scenario, action strategies should fall somewhere between these two extremes. They should include social goals so that in big urban areas a society emerges which is founded on participatory democracy and on "capitalism with a human face" or "market socialism".

But the outlook is less clear than ever. Let us hope the present transition will lead rapidly to a new revival of humanism, whose first signs we are already seeing. This would open up the road to a development which is fair, humane and peaceful.

20

Living with Leviathan

In the year 2015, there will mega-cities with more than 8 million inhabitants—22 of them in Asia. How will they cope? Humanity is about to set a new record. Nearly two-thirds of the planet's population will be living in cities by 2025, UN population experts say. Until now, rural people have outnumbered city-dwellers.

World population, according to the same projections, will top eight billion in 25 year's time, including five billion in cities. The increase will be particularly spectacular in the cities of the developing world, whose total population will double to four billion. We are going to see an unprecedented exodus of people from rural areas.

The demographer's predictions are only tentative of course. But the flow of people into megacities in developing countries is well under way. Several sociological changes are behind it.

Cities used to need muscle-power for the jobs they provided, the experts point out. But today they no longer attract people just because of their economic potential. There is plenty of evidence that they can go on steadily attracting people even when the job-generating sectors are in bad shape or disappearing.

People no longer move to urban centres because they are fairly sure to find work. They do so because they want to leave the countryside where there are too many people tilling the land and because they hope to leave poverty behind. Rightly or wrongly, the city seems to offer progress and freedom, a vision of opportunity, an irresistible lure.

The result is that both inside and outside cities, there are more and more squatters and poor housing. Urbanisation in the developing world differs from that in the industrialised countries, in "the speed of the process, the growth of poverty, the extent of urban sprawl and the expansion of the informal economy."

How are the authorities in the developing world's urban areas responding to such "invasions"? In today's deregulated world, the trend is to question the very idea of providing the general population with basic urban services, most observers note. For want of resources, cities in developing countries are increasingly abandoning their public service function.

China is still an exception to this in several ways. Officials there, in a context of rigid planning—though this has eased in recent years—are trying to prevent the influx of more rural migrants than the city economies can cope with, as the example of Shanghai shows. Can such a policy, which works fairly well for the moment, survive the political and economic hangs under way?

At the other end of the scale is Lagos (Nigeria), whose expansion is chaotic, about 200 slums have sprung up in this African city. Every now and then, one of them is bulldosed without notice and without heed for its inhabitants. But Lagos survives, thanks to the vibrant ingenuity of its millions of citizens. Another revealing city is Jakarta, where the authorities themselves have joined in frantic property speculation. As a result of this speculation, more than 4.5 million people have been evicted from their homes in the last 30 years, with little compensation, to make possible the construction of high-rise blocks, which sometimes stand empty.

How do the original inhabitants of a city react to the

massive influx of people from outside? In more and more cities, you see smart neighbourhood protected by guard—called "fortress-cities". In these fortified enclaves, built partly in response to real or imagined lack of security, the roads, sewage system, schools and other community services are private. Outside them, public areas have been abandoned to the least fortunate members of the society and the infrastructure there is crumbling or inadequate. The middle and poorer classes also defend themselves in their own neighbourhoods. One surprising case can be found in the satellite cities just outside Brasilia, where iron railing protect the houses, from fancy villas to the humblest shack.

Will the mega-cities of the 21st century be made up of islands of "social tribes"- "anticities" of walled enclaves, whose wealthy residents refuse to pay taxes to provide facilities for the city's less fortunate inhabitants? Will cities still integrate their inhabitants?

"The existence of a slum means the authorities have failed," says the World Bank. The bank encourages projects where the state and the private sector join hands to help the less fortunate buy plots of land in areas with an infrastructure. Other experts say the "anti-social" aspects of globalisation should be blamed. They would like to see the big cities of the next century return to their original function as a crossroads and a meeting-place.

21

What is Known About Reducing Maternal Mortality?

Historical records demonstrate the significant improvements that can be achieved when key interventions are in place. Reductions in maternal mortality took place in Sweden during the 1800s, for example, as a result of a national policy favouring professional midwifery care for all births, coupled with establishment of standards for quality of care. By the beginning of the 20th century, maternal mortality in Sweden was the lowest around 230 per 1,00,000 live births compared with over 500 per 1,00,000 in the mid-1880s. In Denmark, Japan, Netherlands, and Norway, similar strategies produced comparable results. In England and Wales, significant reductions in maternal mortality were not apparent until the 1930s; at the national level, political commitment to the strategy was achieved only slowly and the introduction of professional midwifery was correspondingly delayed. In every case, however, the key to these improvements was the institution of fully professional maternity care.

In the USA, where strategy focused on hospital delivery by doctors, maternal mortality remained high because it proved difficult to establish adequate regulatory frameworks and mechanisms to ensure quality of care. In 1930, the maternal mortality ratio in the USA was still 700 per. 1,00,000 live births compared with 430 in England and Wales.

More recently, India witnessed significant reductions in maternal mortality in a relatively short period. From a level of over 1500 per 1,00,000 live births in 1940-1945, maternal mortality fell to 555 per 1,00,000 in 1950-1955, 239 per 1,00,000 within 10 years. And 95 per 1,00,000 by 1980. The figure is now 30 per 1,00,000. These improvements followed the introduction of a system of health facilities around the country allied to an expansion of midwifery skills and the spread of family planning. During the 1950s most births in India took place at home with the assistance of untrained birth attendants. By the end of the 1980s over 85 per cent of all birth were attended by trained personnel.

Similar evidence of the effectiveness of health care interventions is available from China, Cuba, and Malaysia. These countries established community-based maternal health care systems comprising prenatal, delivery, and postpartum care and a system of referral to a higher level of care in the event of obstetric complications.

What these examples clearly demonstrate is that a country's overall economic wealth is not in itself the most important determinant of maternal mortality. There are numerous other examples of countries with modest levels of GNP which have achieved low maternal mortality.

22

Forests

Global losses of forest area have marched in step with population growth for much of human history. The two trends rose slowly for millennia, turned upward in recent centuries, and accelerated sharply after 1900. Indeed, 75 per cent of the historical growth in global population and an estimated 75 per cent of the loss in global forested area have occurred in the twentieth century. The correlation makes sense, given the additional need for farmland, pastureland, and forest products as human numbers expand. But since 1950, the advent of mass consumption of forest products has quickened the pace of deforestation.

In some cases, population pressure is still closely linked with deforestation. In Latin America, for example, ranching is the single largest cause of deforestation. Because most meat produced in Latin America is consumed there, and because meat consumption per person has been largely unchanged for several decades, it is likely that expanding population is the principal reason for ranching-related deforestation. In addition, analysts at the World Resources Institute estimate that overgrasing and overcollection of firewood—which are often a function of a growing population—are degrading some 14 per cent of the world's threatened frontier forests (large areas of virgin forest). In fact, a U.N. Food and Agriculture Organisation study showed a one-to-one correlation between population growth and fuelwood consumption in 16 Asian countries between 1961 and 1994.

On the other hand, deforestation created by the demand for forest products tracks more closely with rising per capita consumption in recent decades, Global use of paper and paperboard per person, for example, has doubled (or nearly tripled) since 1961, and most of the increase has come in wealthy countries with low or even stable levels of population growth. Europe, Japan, and North America, with 16 per cent of global population, consume 63 per cent of the world's paper and paperboard and nearly half its industrial wood.

Although consumption and population growth have operated somewhat independently in the late twentieth century, the two forces could coincide in the developing world in coming decades, with substantial consequences for forests. Developing country paper consumption is less than one tenth the level found in industrial nations, suggesting that large increases in consumption are likely as these nations prosper. (It also suggests that greater economy is needed in industrial countries). With 80 per cent of the world's people, and as home to all the increase in population in coming decades, even modest growth in per capita paper and wood consumption in developing countries could place substantial pressure on forests. If paper were used by the entire world in 2050 at today's industrial-nation rates, paper production would need to jump more than eightfold over 1996 levels.

This projected growth is unsustainable, given that global use of forest products is already near or beyond the limits of sustainable use. Using data on sustainable forest yields, and assuming that virgin forests are left intact, researchers at Friends of the Earth UK have determined that production of forest products for the world is 25 per cent beyond the most restrictive estimates for sustainable consumption. (Many forests, of course, are already logged well beyond sustainable levels). The most optimistic assessment would allow for a further 35 per cent growth in consumption. Even that spells trouble, however, given a projected global population increase of some 54 per cent over the next half-century, and given the likely increase in consumption from rising prosperity. Lower consumption of forest products and increased recycling in industrial countries can make room for a more prosperous developing world to enjoy the products of the world's forests, but the task will be made easier if population growth everywhere is stabilised sooner rather than later.

If population and consumption eat into the world's forests, the resulting loss of forest services reduces, in turn, a country's capacity to support its population. Forests provide habitat to a diverse selection of wildlife; tropical forests, for example, are home to more than 50 per cent of the world's species. And as storehouses of carbon, forests are key to regulating climate. Deforestation leads to huge releases of carbon: an estimated one quarter of the world's carbon emissions come from forest clearing. Loss of these macroservices undermines the stability and resiliency of the global environment on which economies—and populations—depend. In addition, forests provide services vital to a local population, such as control of erosion, steady provision of water across rainy and dry seasons, and regulation of rainfall. Taken together, the loss of these services due to deforestation can upset local economies and subject local populations to economic instability.

23

Meat Production

World meat production increased from 44 million tons almost twice as fast as population. In per capita terms, world meat production expanded from 17 kilograms in 1950 to 36 kilograms in 1997, more than doubling. Growth in meat production was originally concentrated in western industrial countries and Japan, but over the last two decades it has increased rapidly in East Asia (especially China), the Middle East, and Latin America.

When incomes begin to rise in traditional low-income societies, one of the first things people do is diversify their diets, consuming more livestock products. People everywhere appear to have an innate desire to consume at least moderate quantities of meat, perhaps reflecting our evolutionary history as hunter-gatherers.

Three types of meat—beef, pork, and poultry—account for the bulk of world consumption; mutton ranks a distant fourth. From 1950 until 1980, beef and pork production followed the same trend, but after the economic reforms in China—where pork is dominant—pork production surged ahead, climbing from 45 million tons to nearly 90 million tons in less than two decades.

Historically, growth in the world meat supply came primarily from beef and mutton, sustained by the world's rangelands. These areas, consisting mostly of land that is too arid to support crop production, cover a vast part of the planet, roughly double the cropland area. Not only do the herds of cattle and flocks of sheep and goats provide meat and milk, but for millions of people in Africa, the Middle East, Central Asia, parts of the Indian subcontinent, and western China, they provide a livelihood. The only feasible way that this land can contribute to the world's food supply is to graze cattle, sheep, and goats on it, producing the meat and milk that directly and indirectly sustain large segment of humanity.

In recent years, beef and mutton production have levelled off at just over 60 million tons per year as the number of animals has pressed against the carrying capacity of range lands. With little unused grasing capacity left, future gains in meat production will have to come largely from feeding animals grain. At this point, the relative conversion efficiency of various animals begins to influence production trends. Producing a kilogram of beef in the feedlot requires roughly seven kilograms of grain, while a kilogram of pork requires nearly four of grain and a kilogram of poultry, just over two. As grain supplies tighten, the advantage shifts from beef to pork and even more so to poultry. This helps explain why world poultry production overtook that of beef in 1996.

Of the world grain harvest of 1.87 billion tons in 1998, an estimated 37 per cent or nearly 700 million tons—will be used to feed livestock and poultry, producing milk and eggs as well as meat. This share, remarkably stable for the last decade, could go up or down depending on future grain prices.

Expanding world meat production also depends on soyabean production. If the grain fed to livestock or poultry is supplemented with a modest amount of soyabean meal (the high protein meal that is left after the oil is extracted), its conversion into meat is much more efficient. Largely as a result of this growing demand for livestock products, world soyabean production climbed from 17 million tons in 1950 to 152 million tons in 1997, a gain of ninefold.

To project the future demand for meat, we assume that the growth in meat consumption per person will slow over the next half-century, rising by one half instead of doubling, since some countries are nearing the saturation point. This, combined with the projected growth in population, would push total meat consumption from 211 million tons in 1997 to 513 million tons in 2050, a gain of 302 million tons. If we assume an average of 3 kilograms of grain per kilogram of meat produced, this would require more than 900 million tons of additional grain for feed in 2050, an amount equal to half of current world grain consumption. This would greatly intensify the competition between grain consumed directly and that consumed indirectly as animal protein, calling into question whether such gains in meat consumptions will ever materialise.

Grain fed to livestock and poultry is now the principal food reserve in the event of a world food emergency. As of 1990, the world had, in effect, three reserves in the global food system: substantial stocks of grain that could be drawn upon in the event of unexpected shortages, a large area of cropland idled under U.S. farm commodity programmes, and grain fed to animals. By 1998, world grain stocks had been depleted to one of the lowest levels on record and the cropland that was idled for half a century was returned to production. The only safety net remaining in the event of a major crop failure is the grain fed to livestock and poultry.

24

Biodiversity

As human population has surged this century, the populations of numerous other species have tumbled, many to the point of extinction. Indeed, we live amid the greatest extinction of plant and animal life since the dinosaurs disappeared some 65 million years ago, with species losses at 100 to 1,000 times the natural rate. But humans are not just witnesses to a rare historic event, we are actually its cause. The leading sources of today's species loss, habitat alteration, invasions by exotic species, pollution, and overhunting are all a function of human activities.

Human activities have pushed the percentage of mammals, amphibians, land fish that are in "immediate danger" of extinction into double digits. The principal cause of species extinction is habitat loss—the result of encroachment by humans for settlements, for agriculture, or to claim resources such as timber. A particularly productive but vulnerable habitat is found in coastal areas, home to 60 per cent of the world's population. Coastal wetlands nurture two thirds of all commercially caught fish, for example. And coral reefs have the second highest concentration of biodiversity in the world, after tropical rainforests. But human encroachment and pollution are degrading these areas: roughly half of the world's salt marshes and mangrove swamps have been eliminated or radically altered, and two thirds of the world's coral reefs have been degraded, 10 per cent of them "beyond recognition". As coastal migration continues—coastal dwellers could account for 75 per cent of world population within 30 years—the pressures on these productive habitats will likely increase"

Habitat loss tends to accelerate with an increase in a country's population density. This is bad news for the world's biodiversity hotspots-species-rich ecosystems at greatest risk of destruction. Twenty-four of these hotspots, containing half of the planet's species, have been identified globally. Some of the most important hotspot countries will reach population densities that have been linked with very high rates of habitat loss. Five of the six most biologically rich countries could see more than two thirds of their original habitat destroyed by 2050 if this historical relationship holds.

Related to loss of habitat is the growing incidence of plant, animal, insect, and microbial invasions of ecosystems worldwide as human interchange increases. These "exotic species" sometimes dominate local ecosystems, eliminating native species and reducing overall diversity. Exotics are implicated in 68 per cent of all fish exticntions in the United States this century, for example. Growth in human travel and commerce explains many accidental invasions by exotics, but foreign species are also deliberately introduced into farms, plantation forests, and aquaculture systems. Although only 1 per cent of exotics cause widespread damage, exotic species are the second leading cause, after habitat destruction, of species loss worldwide.

Other, often diffuse effects of expanded human activities also disrupt ecosystems. Nitrogen, for example, is now made available to plants at more than twice the preindustrial rate as a result of fertiliser production, cultivation of nitrogen-fixing crops, and the burning of fossil fuels. This overfertilisation of the Earth favours some species at the expense of others, leading to a reduction in diversity and resiliency of land and aquatic ecosystems.

Likewise, greenhouse gas emissions could disrupt ecosystems on a vast scale. As with nitrogen, increased levels of atmospheric carbon may favour some species over others:

annuals over perennials, for example, or deciduous trees over evergreens. To the extent that greenhouse gases induce changes in global climate, many species may be at risk as habitats shift or shrink, and as some life forms, such as insects or animals, adapt and migrate more quickly than others, such as plants. And as sea levels rise with a change in climate, ecosystems such as coastal wetlands could be destroyed.

25

Development

The Third Way

While great claims are being made for the increasingly more efficient and effective technologies perfected to serve development of the people in this scientific age, huge problems are threatening the globe. The problems are mass poverty and hunger, underdevelopment, waste, unemployment, resource scarcity, environmental destruction and armed conflict.

In finding answers to the prevailing problems we must be clear about the meaning and purpose of development. The first glaring mistake made is that development is interpreted as development of the economy and not as the total development of society. When economic development is made the supreme goal, most of the other vital aspects get ignored, namely, development of the political system, community, social cohesion, the ecology, culture and values, development and stability go hand in hand while poverty and chaos constitute the antithetical twin.

Appropriate Development

The key elements in the conception of appropriate development consist of: first, aiming at sufficiently comfortable material living standards and not affluent standards of the rich as in prosperous nations. Second, development must not be confused with GNP growth. Mere increase of economic activity must not be pursued exclusively at the cost of articles that are urgently needed by the poor majority to maintain them at a reasonable level of material living. Third, in the villages, we must produce articles as are needed by the villagers. Fourth grassroots and participatory development is essential so that the local people identify and solve their local problems. Fifth, instead of capital and energy intensive high technology, use labour-intensive technology, instead of heavy indistrialisation, promote medium scale industries and technologies. And, sixth, instead of preoccupation with a high GNP growth rate, focus on the development of communities and of rural bodies and take care to conserve the local ecosystems. The main purpose should be to meet their primary needs of ordinary people and promotion of their productive resources such as land.

In developing countries like India where billions of poor people remain condemned by conventional economic development strategies and theories, it is vital to introduce appropriate development measures to remove deprivation and ensure the necessity of modest living standards.

The world has witnessed the operation of the two systems namely, the capitalist and the socialist one that have obtained in different countries. Although both the systems have underlined the welfare of all as the basic goal, both have left a legacy of waste, hunger and gross human inequality. Some 1000 million people do not get enough to eat including some 20 million in the USA.

Third World Way of Development

The iniquitous situation in the present day world has sparked off fierce controversies among the conventional economists and the new radical economists who champion a third way, as the alternative way to serve the primary goal of all humanity to have sufficient means to lead a comfortable peaceful life.

In order to achieve prosperity, conventional economists have emphasised the production of bigger cake on the assumption that everyone will get a slice of it. They also argue that a "tide will lift all the boats". Both these assumptions have proved false in that the poor have neither the slice of cake nor has their boat been lifted. Third way system lays stress on highly localised, less cash-reliant and simply structured set-up. It should not be dependent on transport of goods, but concentrate on more local production to meet local needs with a role for barter and free exchange. He urges a radical re-think of conventional economics.

Is this Stepping Backwards?

The most common criticism levelled against the Third Way is that it will arrest the progress made hitherto and that it might mean a return to a 'primitive' way of life. There should be no fear on this score because the Third Way aims at the reduction in the use of resources and therefore, of excessive production and consumption. It does not in any sense mean stepping backwards to a lower level of the quality of life. Nor is the alternative way intended to destroy capitalism or socialism. The conception of the alternate way is to promote economic growth compatible with capitalism and socialism. The ground idea is to promote selflessness, mutual concern and social responsibility. This will replace selfish, competitive and avaricious attitudes as have developed in the conventional economic order of today.

NGO's Resolution at the Rio Conference

That there is increasing awareness of the threat posed by the growing power of multinational corporations was articulated by the international NGO forum in its Declaration resolved on 12 June 1992 at the UN Conference of Environment and Development in Rio de Janerio. The Declaration states that "the Bretton Woods institutions have served the major instruments by which the destruction policies have been imposed on the world" and calls upon "the world's people to protect their economic, social, cultural and environmental interests against the growing power of transnational capital". The Declaration further avers "we recognize the central place of spiritual values and spiritual development... and values of simplicity, love, peace, and reverence for life.

After the failure of the socialist system over four decades to achieve prosperity for all, the Indian Government switched over to the global market economy and is steaming ahead with added liberalisation measures to attract foreign investment and the multinational corporations (MNCs). Some adverse effects of this are already visible: for example, majority financial equity granted to MNCs and the emergence of foreign subsidiaries with cent per cent financial equity; the introduction of pizza and Kentucky Fried Chicken which has been detested by the people in Karnataka. The farmers have also revolted because their rights to produce and sell seeds have been wrested by foreign MNCs who have acquired patent rights over certain Indian crop seeds. In this scenario, the Third Way has much to commend itself to the Government. The Third Way has the air of the Gandhian model of economy and production which emphasizes production by people for their own needs and preference for small and medium sized industry. The same paradigm was championed by the renowned economist Schumachar when he said "Small is beautiful". India should take good care against the present-day headlong drive for the entry of foreign capital and foreign heavy industries.

26

Land Tenure

Securing Land for the Urban Poor

Around the world, especially in Asia and Africa, towns and cities are expanding rapidly. For the poorest people, finding affordable, safe and secure urban land for shelter has become increasingly difficult. This is because:

- Overall competition for land makes it increasingly costly:
- Central urban areas are being developed for commercial use;
- Natural features such as mountains or swamps limit physical urban expansion; and
- Meeting land management and planning standards (concerned with legality, technical and administrative accuracy) is expensive.

As a result, a large and increasing proportion of urban populations are forced to live in peripheral areas or occupy marginalised and dangerous locations. These settlements are often illegal and, providing inadequate shelter and lacking essential services only exacerbate the problems of the poor. Higher levels of ill health, unemployment and non-sustainable land-use often result. Furthermore, residents may also be under constant threat of eviction by government and exploitation by landowners.

Experience shows that, if residents in such areas feel secure and safe from eviction, they do over time improve their neighbourhoods. Recognition of, and granting of secure forms of tenure to previously illegal settlements often provides the incentive to communities to invest their resources in upgrading their housing and wider neighbourhoods. Security of tenure also brings the improved likelihood of basic infrastructure and other essential community services.

There is a wide range of urban land tenure systems. In many urban areas, including areas designated illegal by government, there are informal or customary tenure systems—these are often the commonest form of tenure and are expanding most rapidly.

While statutory or "legal" forms of tenure (for example freehold or leasehold agreements) offer many advantages, such as full individual rights and security and access to formal credit systems, they can also cause the very problems they were intended to solve:

- Higher rental levels, which may displace existing renters;
- The selling out of the secure land to higher income groups;
- Encouragement of new illegal/informal settlements, as the poorest hope that they will also eventually get security of tenure;
- Encouragement of landowners and developers to hold land, without investing in its improvement or paying taxes on its increased value—which serves to attract even greater levels of investment and land price inflation.

In addition, if peoples' incomes remain low and the capacity of the banks or credit unions is weak, statutory forms of tenure alone may not necessarily stimulate neighbourhood improvements.

Consequently, careful analysis of existing systems of informal and customary tenure and property rights is required, before embarking on major land management and tenure reforms. These can provide both acceptable levels of security and access to credit, which in turn stimulate improvements to local neighbourhoods. Before any decisions are made, tenure policies must recognise the likely impact on tenants, the poor and other vulnerable groups, especially women.

For these reasons, it is sometimes better to increase the rights of residents (e.g. by protecting them from the threat of forced evictions, or by increasing their access to essential utilities or credit), rather than assuming that they need freehold or leasehold titles.

Strategies for providing shelter now recognise the diverse nature of needs, and the positive contribution which decent housing makes to social and economic development at both national and local levels. They also recognise that the most effective way of mobilising the resources required is to encourage investment in housing by individuals, communities and the private sector.

Recent experience shows that many governments are now introducing positive approaches, which are market-sensitive and encourage more efficient use of available land. These include measures to encourage landowners and developers to allocate a specified proportion of units to low-income groups out of profits generated from planning permission granted by (and therefore partly created by) the government. Public-private partnerships and revisions to planning standards and administrative procedures have also demonstrated that it is possible to reduce the costs of access to land for the poor even under conditions of market-led development, thus reducing urban sprawl, the occurrence of slum settlements and levels of poverty.

27

What's Driving Migration

The scale and diversity of today's migrations are beyond any previous experience. Rapid urban growth and environmental degradation in rural areas have led to internal migration affecting hundreds of millions of people. Migration is now seen as a priority issue equal in political weight to other major global challenges such as the environment, population growth and economic imbalances between regions.

Families and households form the basis for economic growth, social development and personal fulfilment. Decisions, by individual women and men on marriage, family, a place to live, shape the destinies of communities and nations. National policies and international conditions provide the context for individual decision-making. Effective development policies, including population, reproductive health and family planning policies, address this reality.

Data on national and global population trends set the agenda for national policy. An important element of population programmes is gathering data that will allow policy-making responsive to the realities of daily life, and to the needs and aspirations of individuals.

The dominant feature of global demographics is still growth. Age distribution is a growing concern, as the numbers of young and elderly people, grow, relative to the working-age population. The world is growing steadily more urban. From being a sign of strength and dynamism in the national economy, the rate and scale of urban growth has become increasingly a cause for concern. The influx of migrants to the biggest cities may be weakening both urban and rural sectors.

International migration is small in extent compared with internal movements, but has a disproportionate impact. Both internal and international migration are driven by population growth, and by inequities between countries. Migration is one of the choices which shape people's lives and the destiny of nations. But it can also be a symptom of inequity and underdevelopment. Migrants are by definition the most vulnerable members of the host community. Their living and working conditions should be protected.

Open and frank exchange of information and views between host and sending countries is needed more than ever. The aim of the international community should be to protect the right to move, but to ensure that movement is voluntary and that it stimulates rather than holds back personal and national development. "The point of departure should be the human right to live and work where one pleases, so long as it does not infringe on other people's rights to do the same."

The Urban Transformation

The rural sector is declining in importance and its contribution to national economies. It is increasingly part of a unified economy based on the city. Contact with the urban areas is easier than ever and is encouraged by rural development.

Temporary and circular migration is giving way to more permanent settlement. The largest cities are under increasing strain, and residents are encountering increasing difficulties in improving or even maintaining living conditions. Nevertheless, migration continues, driven by a variety of forces both positive and negative. The choice to move can be part of a strategy for survival or personal development; but it is often enforced by external conditions.

The urban transformation is irreversible, but the rural sectors must also be strengthened to balance the developing economy. Attention to gender issues will be crucial in ensuring a successful transition. The forces driving internal and international migration have much in common. Demographic pressures are contributing to both. As the pressures encouraging migration increase, the options for migrants become more limited. This collision is contributing to the atmosphere of crisis surrounding both urban and international migration.

Costs and Benefits

Migration is the result of individual or family decisions. But it is also part of social process. In economic terms, migration is as much a global phenomenon as trade in commodities or manufactured goods. It is part of a broader pattern, and evidence of changing economic, social and cultural relationships.

But migration may be evidence of a different kind of relationship; the combination of poverty, rapid population growth and environmental damage is a powerful destabilising factor driving urban growth and eventually international migration. On the recipient side, migration has usually been seen as evidence of a thriving economy; today's industrial states were built in part by migrant labour, skills and investment. In today's increasingly uncertain conditions, migration may be seen as a threat to the security and well-being of the local workforce and society at large.

The only effective means to reduce migration pressures over the long term are to slow population growth; to stimulate economic growth and job creation at home, and promote the development of the individual and the family as the basic economic and social unit.

A Question of Gender

It is often assumed that most migrants are men, in reality, women make up nearly half of the international migrant population. Gender differences in social and economic roles affect migration decision making, household strategy, and the sex composition of labour migration. Attention to the gender dimension of migratory movements ought to be an important component in population and development planning.

Women frequently take the initiative in migration decisions, which may reflect limited opportunities in rural areas. Low status limits women's choices at home and may increase pressure to migrate, but it may also affect life in the host community. Opportunities may be limited by lack of education or skills, or by customer limitation on women's freedom of action outside the family or ethnic group. Paid employment for migrant women is usually in the lowest wage, least secure, and lowest status jobs, mostly in housework, child care and trade.

Most educated women end up in the same low-status, low-wage production and servicejobs as unskilled female migrants. Men too, experience downward mobility, but the contrast in the decline in women's employment status is far greater. Despite these disadvantages women migrants have become significant economic actors. Their status may be improved by migration, but the advantages are not clear cut. Women's status as migrants is affected by their vulnerability, and by their lack of reproductive freedom. To ensure improved status they will need both legal protection and essential services, including reproductive health services.

Refugees

Refugees in the 1990s are overwhelmingly in Asia, Africa and Latin America. Their numbers are large, about 17 million, and growing rapidly. A further 3.5 to 4 million were thought to be in "refugee-like situations", though estimates are probably extremely conservative, and an estimated 23 million people internally displaced.

It is important to recognize the common roots of refugees and other forms of mass movement of populations.

At the same time, despite the difficulty of distinguishing between political and socio-economic causes of migration, there is a clear need to distinguish between refugees and other groups of migrants. Participation in international efforts of burden-sharing would ensure that most refugee problems would be dealt with in their regions of origin.

Conclusions and Policies

Migration highlights linkages and interdependencies within countries, with many implications for development agendas, including population programmes and development assistance.

Policies to regulate or moderate international migration have concentrated largely on urban growth. They have been only intermittently effective. The most successful have concentrated on stimulating rural development and the growth of alternative urban centres.

Migration is also a personal or family decision, which is affected by external conditions such as poverty or environmental degradation, improving conditions of personal and family life can make a crucial difference in the decision to migrate, reducing dependence on migration as a strategy. Because migration is the result of personal and family decisions, it can be influenced by policies that improve the quality of life.

This offers the opportunity for policies emphasising individual development, among them education, health (including reproductive health) and family planning. Such policies are particularly relevant to the strategies must take into account gender differences in social and economic life and the differential effects of policies.

Migration decisions are about family security and long-term-life-chances, rather than simply the maximisation of income. They are ultimately strategies designed to look after the individual's and the household's needs, safeguard their security, and respond to their aspirations. If the goal is to reduce migration pressures through development it will be essential to increase the capacity but reduce the need to migrate. Long-term external support will be required to make such policies a reality, particularly in areas of rapid population growth and potential mass outward flows. Highly co-ordinated allocation of development assistance can be help establish priorities and focus attention on basic needs. The challenge to both international donors and co-operating governments is to direct programme spending to the areas where it can be most effective.

28

Resistance to Change

Why Poverty Reduction Programmes did not Work

Poverty reduction as an overall objective of the global development industry is not new. The only problem is that so far it has not really worked. Despite several decades of economic growth and huge development aid disbursements, the number of countries the United Nations calls "least developed" (those with a per capita income of less than US$ 900 a year) has in fact nearly doubled since 1971, from 25 to 49. In the last decade (1990-2000) and despite all development efforts—not even one country was able to graduate from this group to a higher income level, may be with the exception of Botswana.

Meanwhile, poverty reduction has generated its own history. This programme has covered a wide range of approaches starting from the World Banks's small-farmers-strategies in the 1970s via the costly structural adjustment policies of the 1980s to the recent poverty reduction strategies of the 1990s. Once more, the next development decade (2000-2010) has written "Attacking Poverty" on its banner. It seems that something must have gone wrong along the way. What (bitter?) lessons have been learnt from previous experience? Have they been factored into the new set of policies? Were there possibly some fundamental flaws which were overlooked, and can better results be expected during the next period? Or do the many failures and disappointments demonstrate that there is some systemic "resistance to change" by those in power in the least developed countries and perhaps also by the poor themselves?

1. What can the Rural Poor Really Expect from Poverty Reduction Programmes?

In India, of example, 70 per cent of the people still earn their livelihood in the agricultural sector; most of the poor among them live in a kind of rural subsistence economy. People who live in a subsistence economy are naturally conservative. They are busy securing their survival and are very reluctant to take risks. Their living standard is measured in amounts of rice harvested; their wealth is measured in numbers of livestock. Within this simple framework, poor peasants behave very rationally. For example, a shift from food crops to cash crops, such as from rice to coffee or tapioca, would immediately endanger their subsistence in case of failure. Furthermore, the poor do not have the knowledge and skills to change their crops quickly in response to market demands. Moving from a subsistence economy to a commodity economy is therefore a big step for small farmers.

However, poor people are always happy to receive handouts from the Government like fertiliser, seeds, medicine or blankets. Roads, bridges and schools are also very welcome. Who would refuse a gift? From their point of view, it is the responsibility of the Government to distribute goods and services in the form of aid programmes as a way to share some of the prosperity of the city people with them. Nevertheless, as they see no direct and immediate benefit for themselves, they tend to take a rather passive attitude to change. Development workers have often complained about this common apathy and about the lack of will among the poor themselves to improve their situation. In the final analysis, rural development is more a problem of providing the right economic incentives for change than of overcoming traditional thinking and a conservative attitude.

2. What Kind of Incentives are Necessary to Achieve Increased Production in the Countryside?

In most poor countries the key to rural development is the problem of land ownership rights and of legal security. As long as people do not own the land that they cultivate, they are not interested in making any investments, be they in the form of labour or capital. Once a farmer has an ownership title and considers the land as his own, he will refrain from overusing the soil but shift crops and plant new trees. Moreover, he can then use his land as collateral for credits or even sell it and buy land somewhere else.

In addition to clear and irrevocable ownership rights, the rule of law is another crucial factor for development. People must feel safe from abuse of power by local elites and corrupt government officials. They must be able to enforce their basic rights in an impartial court of law. Furthermore, they must be safe from land expropriation without adequate compensation and from resettlement against their will. In other words, it is primarily their very stake holdership in the rural economy that will motivate them to increase their production. Of course, the other necessary incentives are access to markets, a fair price for their products and the availability of goods and services.

3. Poverty Reduction Programmes, if not accompanied by Parallel Institutional Reforms, run the risk of creating a Modern Version of the Cargo Cult

Cargo cults spread during World War II in the highlands of Papua New Guinea at a time when several US cargo planes loaded with food supplies crashed into the hills. Suddenly, the native people could enjoy an abundant amount of goods, which literally fell down on them like a "gift from heaven". In the hope of attracting some more of these "silvery birds", the local hill-tribes constructed primitive models of airplanes, sat around them in a circle, and prayed that more "cargo" would drop on their territory. As this happened in some areas (albeit as a result of the air battle between Japan and the USA), it strengthened the belief in the cargo cult as some magical way to overcome poverty—at least for a short time.

There is a high risk that aid programmes under the banner of poverty reduction will create new "cargo cults" in the 49 least developed countries if they continue to carry out their "business as usual" and do not put strong emphasis on the rule of law and civil rights. Unfortunately, the setting up of reliable legal and social institutions in poor countries (which often seems to be the "software" of the development industry accompanying disbursements) is, in fact, as decades of experience have shown, the hard part of the process. But it is also indispensable for achieving any tangible results.

Why have there been until now only modest results in the areas of land reform, rule of law and the guarantee of basic civil rights? Why have people's participation and people's ownership as a strategy hardly taken root at all in the least developed countries? The answer must be sought in the role of powerful local groups and their vested interest, who obviously benefit from the prevailing status quo and a loose legal environment. A cargo cult promises bounty for all recipients; poverty reduction, however, means changing the rural power structure, too.

Conclusion

To insist on the rule of law, on people's participation in the development process, and on transparency and accountability, is again nothing new. Good political and administrative institutions go hand in hand with economic growth. The potential of economic development is quite limited if it works in a framework of social undevelopment and official indifference. Again the question is, who has so little been achieved in this field during previous decades? Was it the wrong medicine and why were the poor results of the aid programmes so carefully ignored by the international donor community?

Looking at the political systems of the 49 least developed countries, it is obvious that most of these countries are "more democratic in principle than in practice". Many of them are ruled by military or civil authoritarian regimes which are more used to giving orders than to listening to the grievances of the poor, Other governments, such as India, are "genuinely democratic at most levels but have historically found it difficult that political accountability reaches all levels of decision-making, particularly for the poor."

To sum up, it seems that resistance to change is equally shared by the cumbersome and often incompetent bureaucracies of the poor countries and the equally cumbersome international donor community, which has so far conveniently kept the call for more rural democracy and people's rights on the backburner. The major reason for the reluctance of the donor community to pursue the battle for the rule of law and the fight against endemic corruption was to avoid massive political confrontation with the receiver countries.

Would it not have been better to create proper incentives for the performance of poor countries, namely by halting loans to nations that do not manage their economies and their reform commitments effectively and increasing financial and technical support to those that do? The next decade will show how determined both local governments and donors are to tackle these problems for the sake of a better future.

29

Unemployment in the Poor and Rich Worlds
Different Causes, but Converging Policies?

In view of the magnitude of global unemployment, all the customary formulas offered by economists against mass unemployment—the basic socio-economic problem of modern times—appear to be quackery. Neither quantitative, nor any kin of 'qualitative', growth will be able to eliminate the disastrous worldwide lack of jobs. For ecological reasons it is impossible to include 800 million or more unemployed in the production process through corresponding growth. The resulting increase in global Gross Domestic Product would require consumption of natural resources, energy and the environment which, given even the greatest possible productivity in those sectors, could not even be sustained for two or three decades.

In addition, aiming to achieve full employment through growth will be even more difficult even in the rich economies. For it is most likely that work productivity will continue to rise worldwide. Countries such as China, which are in the initial phase of modernisation, are still producing at a relatively still low productivity rate. But that is precisely why they can achieve notable increases in productivity in a short time by importing technology from highly-developed countries. The advantage of rapid 'catch-up rationalisation', however, is being bought at the cost of rising unemployment and progressive impoverishment.

Employment through Redistribution of Work

The notion that jobs can at some time be created for 800-900 million unemployed who will work 35 or even 40 hours a week at the productivity level of the highly-developed countries of four or five decades ago is absurd. The only realistic possibility of eliminating the world's unemployment problem is by far-reaching redistribution of work and income. The change needed for that demands fundamentally new concepts of prosperity: a reflection on the philosophy of the 'life of happiness'. 'New concepts of prosperity' means that technological progress would no longer be used mainly to deliver rising per capita incomes and excessive consumption. Instead, given a sufficient material standard of living, the quality of life would be improved primarily by shortening working hours. It is about, so to speak, assigning instrumental good sense new goals. Plus reshaping socio-economic conditions in such a way that the politicians will again be compelled to orient themselves on the good of the community and humanistic values instead of filling the pockets of the wealthy. It is sheer ideology, although very persuasive, to cite 'globalisation' and its alleged 'iron laws' in defaming the welfare state, full employment and social justice as out-of-date wishful thinking. A return to the state-guided social competitive system as practised during the first decades after the Second World War is possible just as it was politically feasible to make the transition from the old order of unfettered, ruthless capitalism to the mixed economies of the social market economy types. So it is a matter of restoring the proven structures of a mixed economic system.

However, in contrast to the first postwar decades it is now not sufficient to regenerate nation-sate interventionism. Appropriate international regualtions are required. Above all, it will depend upon reversing the new laissez-faire developments in international economic relationships which today are subsumed under the buzzword 'globalisation'. That is, to oppose over-liberalisation and its disastrous social and inhuman impacts. It will depend on the broad mobilisation of the losers in the process of globalisation whether the necessary fundamental change of course can still be made in time before a catastrophe. In particular, the new myth must be opposed that declares globalisation as a kind of law of nature and thus suggests resignation and adaptation to an allegedly unavoidable process of destruction of social and human achievements.

Mass Unemployment in the Poor Economies

The employment problems in the rich and the poor hemispheres differ not only in their magnitude, but also in their causes. The wretched condition of the poor economies is due above all to historical reasons: colonialism and, in the post-colonial era, the constraints to independent development imposed by the hegemonic influence of the rich industrial states. The waste of scarce resources by international and civil wars, and the dictatorships with their upperclass luxury consumption and inefficient, thus development—obstructing exploitation structures—often supported by the industrialised nations—have for a long time repressed and in many cases destroyed autonomous development potential. The colonial and post-colonial distortion also contributed at least indirectly to the current population problems of the poor countries. The politically inflicted mass poverty and under-development stabilised or in fact brought about economic, socio-psychological and ideological mechanisms which oppose an effective population policy. As we know, the average educational level in many developing countries, especially among women, is too low to give a modern population policy a chance of success. Mass unemployment in the poor countries is the result of poverty. In this respect, it is about a production-side problem: to few resources, to little real and human capital, and the inefficient, unproductive use of much of the anyway limited added value of society. The picture is totally different in the rich countries—the over-production economies.

Unemployment in Over-Production Systems

The main cause of mass unemployment in the

industrialised nations has nothing to do with shortages. It is a phenomenon of surplus. Greater possibilities of production can no longer be used 'sufficiently' profitably because the required demand is lacking. Production is done for profit. The necessary collateral condition is the satisfying of consumer needs. Employment is not even such a condition, but only a side effect which lapses immediately when labour-free production is technically possible. Thus, national income must be shared among wages and profits (or income from property). Profit is the difference between earnings and costs. Earnings depend upon demand. Macroeconomic costs consist mainly of wages and salaries (including social security contributions). These definitive connections mean that profit can be made only if overall demand is greater than the total cost labour. But in the final analysis this demand can only come from the profit-earners themselves. In his book, a Treatise on Money, Keynes described this nexus as the theory of the Widow's cruse. Under capitalistic conditions, labour is only sought or hired if profit can be earned with it. But as making a profit depends upon the demand for consumption and investment by the shareholders, it can be seen that the degree of employment is determined by the demand behaviour of the class that receives income from property. In this respect, the widespread belief that greater investment also leads to more employment, namely via the effect of investment in demand, is right.

Lower Wages Mean Lower Demand

The lower the level of wages, and given an unchanged total demand, the greater are the profits that can be made. But it is more likely that in the case of falling wages the overall demand will also drop. For stabilising total demand would require the recipients of income from property to increase their spending on consumption and/or investment to the degree to which wages and the consumption based on them fell.

During the last 10 to 15 years the development of profits in most industrialised nations has been very favourable. But profits would have grown more strongly if the demand of the shareholder had been much greater. This would have created more employment at the same time. Thus, it can be assumed that the profits are simply too high for the shareholders to be able to go in for meaningful consumption or make profitable investments. That is the reason for the extreme redirection of capital from fixed assets to portfolio investment. The growth of speculative (unproductive) financial transactions during the 1980s and 1990s (buzzword: casino capitalism), corresponded with a relatively weak formations of real capital.

Wage rises, of course, narrows the scope for profit. But precisely this effect stimulated efforts to improve the profit situation not only by investment in rationalisation, but also by investment in expansion aimed at the growing mass purchasing power. Since more is being invested, the profit mass also is growing according to the principle of the Widow's cruse. Too low wages, as it were, relieve the shareholders of the pressure to innovate and invest and allow them to earn their profits too easily. That is the real message of the 'purchasing power theory' of wages.

Over-Accumulation and Under-Consumption

Overproduction has two different causes which, however, mostly occur in tandem. They are over-investment, or creation of over-capacities, on the one hand, and lack of demand due to relative saturation and an absence of mass purchasing power on the other. But the main reason for mass unemployment in the rich hemisphere currently lies on the demand side. During the first three decades after the Second World War supply and demand rose in relative balance. Economic fluctuations showed up as temporary declines in generally positive GDP growth rates. These decades of (dynamic) balance of growth are often described today as the era of 'Fordism'. Its essential feature is that rising wages ensure continuing growth of consumption, so that equally growing profits also flow relatively continuously into investments to expand capacity and create jobs. The label

'Fordism' expresses the 'simple' view of the theory for the buying power of wages which is said to have been propagated by Henry Ford I. This was that his workers should earn enough to be able to buy the cars they made.

The astonishingly balanced development of supply and demand from 1950 to the mid-1970s was due above all to postwar reconstruction and the pent-up demand of consumers who were starved by wartime economy shortages. This stimulated positive investment sentiment, and high investments brought at the same time high profits. The postwar growth that led within a short time to full employment was also linked with growth in productivity, which on multi-year average was more than twice that of the crisis period of the last 25 years. Thus, the so-called employment threshold (the GDP growth rate point at which employment growth begins) was much higher in those days than it is now, although there was full employment over a longer period. This simple fact opposes the thesis often propounded today that mass unemployment is above all related to rationalisation. Its is not rationalisation per se, that is, progress that boosts productivity, which is the evil. The problem is that the mistakes in distribution policy which are rooted in capitalistic structures result in increases in supply encountering insufficient demand for goods, whereby the demand for labour drops. However, the fact that demand policy contradicts the requirements of a social ethic that is ecologically responsible and right for the interests of the poor countries was already spelled out. So if a demand—oriented growth policy is practised at all, it should be designed to be as environmentally compatible as possible. After all, there are possibilities for that, such as by expanding the production of services that spares resources. A one-hour driving lesson costs more energy than one hour of ballet instruction.

The politically initiated and implemented over-liberalisation and surrender of social prosperity to global competition since the 1970s, which reproduces the old self-destructive mechanism of laissez faire, have during the last two decades markedly accelerated the crisis development inherent in the system.

Summing Up, it is Noted that

- full employment in the rich economies would certainly be possible by means of demand policy, but only at a high cost to the environment that is concomitant with high growth rates;
- the growth policy of the rich countries impairs the poor economies' possibilities of medium to long-term growth, since these are falling back ever further in the competition for ever scarcer and thus ever more expensive resources;
- the environmental collapse currently expected for the third or fourth generation after us, which obviously also will trigger a collapse of the world economy and—probably ahead of that—armed conflicts which today are hardly imaginable, would happen very much sooner if economic growth were to be increased to such a degree that it would bring full employment worldwide;
- in the long term, the problem of global unemployment and global poverty can only be solved by a policy of massive redistribution, and in fact a redistribution of work and income, whereby increases in productivity must be used mainly or only for shortening working hours. That is a demand, which appears to be utopian. But utopias of today often have the quality of scripting the reality of tomorrow.

30

Third World Debt is Still Growing

Developing country debt is estimated to have grown to over $ 1.8 trillion last year, up from $1.77 trillion in 1994. During the past decade, much of this debt has been restructured-renegotiated on terms more favourable to debtor countries. Some 80 per cent of the funds owed to commercial banks, as well as a much smaller share of loans from governments and multilateral institutions, have now been restructured. The trend has led some analysts to declare the debt crisis over, at least for the private banks. But the poorest nations have yet to see much relief. Their debt service payments still eat up a substantial percentage of their export revenues—some 15 to 19 per cent, depending upon the measurements used. The ratio typical of the era before the crisis began in 1982 was on the order of 10 to 12 per cent.

The worst debt today is that of Sub-Saharan Africa, excluding South Africa. Collectively the region's debt amounts to $ 180 billion, three times the 1980 total, and 10 per cent higher than its entire output of goods and services. Debt service payments come to $10 billion annually, about four times what the region spends on health and education combined. The burden is choking off economic development over much of the continent.

Eastern Europe and the countries of the former Soviet Union are also heavily indebted, but the picture varies considerably from one country to another. The region's total debt rose from 161 per cent of export earnings in 1986 to an estimated 291 per cent last year. Russia owes over $80 billion, and the country is hard pressed to meet its obligations: interest payments in 1994 were budgeted at less than 15 per cent of interest due. Poland, on the other hand, had 40 per cent of its debt forgiven in a restructuring agreement last year. Half of Bulgaria's debt was forgiven in 1993.

In Latin America, restructuring has eased the burdens of three major borrowers—Mexico, Argentina, and Brazil. Peru is the region's last remaining country with significant unrestructured debt. Peru's debt currently amounts to $26 billion.

Restructuring has brought some new actors onto the scene—and changed the roles of established players. After shedding much of the "old", high-risk debt of the 1980s, the commercial banks are moving aggressively into lucrative East Asian markets, and into private sector lending in Latin America. This more selective lending has allowed American banks, for instance, to post a 17 per cent increase in Third World loans over the year ending last March, and a 33 per cent increase since 1990.

As private lending goes elsewhere, the poorest countries have had to rely increasingly on multilateral institutions like the World Bank and the International Monetary Fund. Multilateral debt among the lowest income countries grew from around 15 per cent of total debt in 1980s to over 24 per cent in 1992. Multilateral loans generally come with much stricter terms. Neither the World Bank nor the IMF will directly forgive or restructure debt, since that might jeopardize their "preferred status" in capital markets and force them to raise interest rates. Their preferred status also means that payments to these institutions take precedence over payments to all other creditors. Of the various types of external debt, multilateral loans generally have the most rigid terms.

The multilaterals do, however, participate in a form of restructuring by providing most of the financing for "Brady" bonds, used to restructure the old debt of "middle income" countries like brazil, Mexico, and Argentina. But the bonds are not available to the poorest countries.

Organisations that aren't in the business of lending money have become involved in restructuring as well, through swap agreements. Debt swaps reduce the amount owed in return for some concession on the debtor. In debt-for-equity swaps, for example, a corporation purchases a debtor nation's IOU from a band, and then trades it for one of the country's state-owned assets, such as a steel mill or a telephone company Debt-or equity swaps are often part of a larger privatisation strategy, especially in Latin America. While privatisation may often be necessary for saving nationalised industries, many observers are concerned that indebtedness is forcing countries to part with their assets at "fire sale" prices. Between 1985 and 1992, debt-for-equity swaps accounted for nearly 36 per cent of all debt conversions.

Debt-for-nature and debt-for-development swaps are intended to win government commitments to environmental and development projects. In these arrangements, a non governmental organisation (NGO) usually obtains the debtor nation's IOU from a bank at a significant discount. The NGO then typically restructures the debt by passing along some of the discount conceded by the bank, accepting payments in local currency, and investing the returns locally, to fund a national part, for instance, or a public health project. Between 1985 and 1992, these types of swaps accounted for only about 2 per cent of debt conversions. But for some countries, they may already be offering significant relief: Madagascar has cut its $100 million commercial bank debt in half through debt-for-nature swaps.

31

The Nature and Causes of Drug Addiction

Man has been experimenting for thousands of years with a variety of naturally occurring substances that act on his nervous tissues: alcohol to intoxicate a weary mind, belladonna to calm an angry intestine or to poison an adversary, opium to overcome worry and strain. The relief of pain, in particular, in an age-old aim of mankind, and various narcotic and sleep-producing agents were probably used by primitive man. But for many men there is another kind of pain—the pain of being—and from time immemorial some men have been trying to expand their vision, enhance their appreciation of their world, change their mood, alter their inner existence, or stupefy their awareness with such drugs as alcohol, opium, and cannabis.

Drugs, chemical substances that affect the functions of living things, are used in treating, preventing and diagnosing diseases. The most important source of drugs today is chemical synthesis. The increase in the manufacture of drugs has resulted in the development of 25,000 or more drug and drugs products. Many drugs are potentially dangerous chemicals that can cause serious, sometimes fatal, poisoning if used incorrectly: governments of various countries, therefore, have established certain legal requirements concerning drug use.

Uses: The main purpose of the use of drugs is to cure disease or correct a disorder. Chemotherapeutic drugs, such as the antibiotics, the sulfa drugs, and the antimalarial drugs, fight infection by acting directly on disease causing invading organisms, either immobilising or killing them. Some chemotherapeutic drugs are also used to suppress or prevent infection.

Drug Toxicity

No drug is free of toxic effects. This factor is what ultimately limits the usefulness of drugs. Some of the untoward effects of drugs are trivial and can be readily tolerated. Others, however, are serious and may even be fatal. Some toxic effects of drug are merely extension of the drug's therapeutic effects.

This is why drugs never should be taken except under the guidance of a physican. A physician is aware of the potential hazards of a drug and is prepared to act promptly if toxicity occurs. Furthermore, the physician is aware that many of the toxic effects produced by drugs are unexpected, bizarre, and often not clearly related to the taking of a drug.

Many people suffer from drug allergy—one of the most serious problems of pharmacology. Penicillin, for example, is an extremely safe drug for most people, but it produces hypersensitivity reactions in about 15 per cent of the population. In some cases the reaction is so serious that is necessary to forbid the future use of penicillin because of the risk of death. Drug allergy takes many different forms; skin reactions varying from a mild rash to severe dermatitis.

Drug Addiction and Abuse. It is very likely that every society has had mood-changing drug and that there have always been individuals who used them in ways that were not socially approved. In this sense, drug abuse, the socially nonsanctioned use of a drug, is universal and so old as history. Which behaviours are called drug abuse varies from culture to culture and from time to time within the same culture. Since laws do not always correspond to prevalent social attitudes, there may be times when users of an illegal drug are not considered to be drug abusers.

From a pharmacological viewpoint, attitudes toward drugs are often inconsistent or irrational. Some drugs may be totally outlawed, while others with similar actions are made generally available and may be self-administered with full social approval.

The repeated use of some drugs can lead be a dependence on the drug, in which the effects of the drug or the conditions associated with its use are felt by the users to be necessary for their well being. Dependence may vary in intensity from a mild inclination to a strong craving or compulsion to use the drug. Severe dependence may result in a type of behaviour is also known as Compulsive drug use, and since a severe dependence on any self-administered drug is generally not socially approved, the term is usually synonymous with compulsive drug abuse. One obvious exception is the use of tobacco, where social acceptance is so complete that even heavy compulsive use which is damaging to the user's health, is commonly not considered to be drug abuse.

The term drug addiction has been defined in many ways, but in this article it is used to mean a behavioural pattern of compulsive drug use characterised by an overwhelming involvement with the procurement and use of the drug and the high tendency of the user to relapse to drug use after a period of abstinence. It is synonymous with intensive or severe drug dependence. Contrary to popular belief, drug addiction is not same as physical dependence on a drug. Physical dependence is a physiological or biochemical condition produced by the administration of a drug to the extent that a characteristic pattern of signs and symptoms appears when the drug is withdrawn and disappears when the drug is administered again. Physical dependence can be produced by a wide variety of drugs that are used in everyday medical practice. Some drugs that produce physical dependence are not pleasant to take and are neither abused nor used compulsively. Also, not all withdrawal symptoms are associated with a craving for the drug that produced the physical dependence.

The Nature and Causes of Drug Addiction

If opium were the only drug of abuse, and the only kind of abuse were one of habitual, compulsive use, discussion of addiction might be a simple matter. But opium is not the only drug of abuse, and there are probably as many kinds of abuse as there are drugs to abuse, or indeed, as may be there are persons who abuse. Various substances are used in so many different ways by so many different or one definition could possibly embrace all the medical, psychiatric, psychological, sociological, cultural, economic, religious, ethical, and legal considerations that have an important bearing on addiction. Prejudice and ignorance have led to the labeling of all use of nonsanctioned drugs as addiction and of all drugs, when misused, as narcotics. The continued practice of treating addiction as a single entity is dictated by custom and law, not by the facts of addiction.

Many substances are capable of acting on biological systems, and whether a particular substance comes to be considered a drug depends, in large measure, upon whether it is capable of eliciting a "drug like" effect that is valued by the user. There is nothing intrinsic to the substances themselves that sets one active substance is imparted to it by use. Caffeine, nicotine, and alcohol are clearly drugs, and the habitual excessive use of coffee, if not addiction. The same could be extended to cover tea, chocolates, or powdered sugar, if society wished to use and consider them that way. The task of defining addiction, then is the task of being able to distinguish between opium and powdered sugar while at the same time being able to embrace the fact that both can be subject to abuse. This requires a frame of reference that recognizes that almost any substance can be considered a drug, that almost any drug is capable of abuse, that one kind of abuse may differ appreciably from another kind of abuse, and that the effect valued by the user will differ from one individual to the next for a particular drug, or from one drug to the next drug for a particular individual. This kind of reference would still leave unanswered various questions of availability, public sanction, and one kind of effect rather than another at a particular moment in history, but it does at least acknowledge that drug addiction is not a unitary condition.

Effect on the Mind and Body. The effects of drugs similar in many ways to those of alcohol. Low doses usually produce relaxation and decreases anxiety; higher doses produce drowsiness. Even if people can stay awake, they may appear confused and show poor judgement and loss of emotional control. Slurred speech, a staggering gait, muscular incoordination and nystagmus (rapid involuntary eye movements) are also characteristic effects. Although alcohol and the sedative-hypnotics are all depressants of the nervous system, low or moderate doses can produce an effect that resembles stimulation. The individual may become euphoric and more active, and show a decrease in inhibitions. Very high doses produce coma and death due to respiratory failure.

Drugs In Psychiatry. Drugs that are used either alone or in conjunction with psychotherapy to treat psychiatric illness. The medical treatment of psychiatric illness is based on a firm conviction that the patient's behaviour is in fact a symptom of an illness and not simply a variant of acceptable behaviour in society. The study of drug effects on mental processes is called psychopharmacology.

Certain patterns of disease with mental manifestations are biologically characteristic of humans. The use of drugs to treat these disease patterns is directed either at alleviating symptoms or at inhibiting or stopping the underlying disease processes. Diseases that have purely psychological causes, but appear in ways that disturb society or distress the individual, are often treated with nonspecific remedies, that either sedate or alert the individual. For all mental illness with specific biological causes, psychopharmacologists seek to develop drugs that change the biological functioning of the individual so that the symptoms of disease either do not occur or have a lesser impact on his or her life and behaviour.

The use of drugs in the treatment of psychiatric illness is not a denial of the importance of psychological or social factors in the causation or pattern of a disease. Drug treatment of psychiatric illness is based on the principle that the human nervous system is always a chemical biological system. Some psychiatric treatment system—for example, psychoanalysis—do not utilise drug treatment. Some mental health experts feel that the use of drugs is only for the control of patients and not their treatment.

Social and Ethical Issues of Drug Use

Conflicting Values in Drug Use

The social and economic requirements of modern society may have undergone a radical change in the last few decades, even though the inertia of the existing social character, its desires and its values, will be felt for some time to come. In one major sense, current drug controversies are a reflection of this cultural lag with all of the consequent conflict of wishes and values that result of the consequent conflict of wishes and values that result from the lack of good correspondence between traditional teachings and the view of the world as it is now being perceived by large numbers within society. Modern society is in a state of rapid transition, and this transition is not without its untoward consequences in terms of stability.

Cultural transitions notwithstanding, the dominant social order has strong negative feelings about any nonsanctioned use of drugs that contradicts its existing value system. Can society succeed if individuals are allowed unrestrained self-indulgence? Is it bad to rely on something so much that one cannot exist without it? Is it legitimate to take drugs if one is not sick? Does one have right to decide for oneself what one needs? Does society have the right to punish someone if he has done no harm to himself or to others? These are difficult questions that do not admit to ready answers. Once can guess what the answers would be to the nonsanctioned use of drugs. The traditional ethic dictates harsh responses to conduct that is "self-indulgent" or "abusive of pleasure." But how does one account for the quantities of the drugs being manufactured and consumed today by the general public? It is one thing to talk of the few hundred thousand or so "hard" narcotic users who are principally addicted to the opiates. One might still feel comfortable in disparaging the widespread illicit use of hallucinogenic substances; these are still the "other guys". But the sedatives, tranquilisers, sleeping remedies, stimulants, alcohol, coffee, tea, and tobacco are complications that trap the advocate in some glaring inconsistencies. It may be asked by partisans whether the cosmetic use of stimulants for weight control is any more legitimate than the use of stimulants to "get with it?"; whether the conflict-ridden businessman or the conflict-ridden housewife is any more entitled to relax chemically (alcohol, tranquilisers, sleeping aids, sedatives) than the conflict-ridden adolescent?"; Whether physical pain is any less bearable than mental pain or anguish? Billions of pills and capsules of a nonnarcotic type are manufactured yearly.

Sedatives and tranquilisers account for somewhere around 12 to 20 per cent of all doctor's prescriptions. In addition there are about 150 different sleeping aids that are available for sale without a prescription. The alcoholic beverage industry produces countless millions of gallons of wine and spirits and countless millions of barrels of beer each year. One might conclude that there is a whole drug culture; that the problem is not confined to the young, the poor, the disadvantaged, or even to the criminal' that existing attitudes are at least inconsistent, possibly hypocritical. One always justifies one's own drug use, but one tends to view the other fellow who uses the same drugs as an abuser who is weak and undesirable. It must be recognised that the social consensus in regard to drug use and abuse is limited, conflict ridden, and often glaringly inconsistent. The problem is not one of insufficient facts but one of multiple objectives that at the present moment appear unreconcilable.

32

Not Yet Fossil Fuel

People were gathering wood for their fires more quickly than it could grow back. In India, wood was being burned 50 per cent faster than replacement trees were growing. Among environmentalists, the perception became widespread that village cooking fires were consuming the Indian forest.

Firewood demand was a minor cause of deforestation. People were mostly using twigs and dead branches for fuel, leaving trees standing. The main perpetrators of deforestation were not women preparing for the evening meal, but farmers clearing land for crops and livestock. To this day, however, the belief persists that fuelwood scarcity drives deforestation. That popular misconception has hampered efforts to address serious fuelwood problems that do exist. While not quite deforesting the globe, these problems are undermining the well-being of millions of people in India.

Until recently, most biomass consumer lived in rural areas. As populations have grown, and the number of trees has diminished, searching for fuelwood has indeed become a demanding task. In some areas of India, for example, collecting firewood was a two-hour task only a generation ago, yet today it is almost an entire day's expedition—every day. That constitutes an enormous erosion of productivity in other kinds of work. And the problem is worsening rapidly.

What makes the situation even more difficult is that fuel-wood problems have now spread from rural areas to the cities. In the 1950s, the cities in India were relatively small, inhabited mainly by those who could afford such "modern" fuels as kerosene, liquefied petroleum gas (LPG), and electricity. But in the past three decades, urban populations have exploded as migrants from the rural areas pour into the cities in search of jobs and higher standards of living.

Despite the availability of the "modern" energy sources to some of the city dwellers, the majority of migrants cannot afford them. Wood remains their fuel. But instead of collecting it, they now must buy it from vendors.

Biomass traders search for wood in communal woodlots, and consequently procure lit as a "free" commodity. The price of the wood, which represents only the transport costs and traders markups, excludes the production and replacement costs—at the expense of rural people and the natural resource base. After decades of woodland exploitation in some areas of India, the shortage of firewood in rural areas has become so severe that villagers are compelled to use cow dung, dried leaves, and grass for fuel. The fragile soils of the farmlands are thus denied essential nutrients and organic matter.

Villagers are working hard to reduce the exploitation of their resource base by the urban entrepreneurs. For example, in a village not far from the capital city of Delhi, residents decided to charge traders for wood taken from their communal land. Extension agents were brought in to train the villagers in negotiating wood prices, maintaining accounts, and establishing an agro-forestry project. The revenue from wood sales is now used by the villagers to plant trees that will not only provide fuel for their personal use and for sale, but can be used for other purposes such as construction.

Dependence on wood for fuel is not just a challenge to economic sustainability, but also a threat to Indians health. In the homes of low-income families, where traditional wood stoves are widely used for cooking, adequate ventilation is often lacking. These stoves require large quantities of wood, are unable to retain heat for prolonged periods, and send much of the fuel up in smoke. Inhaled by women as they cook, the smoke has been identified as a major cause of respiratory problems such as bronchitis, and of damaged eyesight.

Improved wood and charcoal stoves are now for sale in India. Because they require significantly smaller quantities of firewood or charcoal, they are successfully curbing the wood demand, and hence promoting biomass conservation.

In the cities, as vendors travel longer distances into the hinterland in search of wood, and the transportation costs increase, more of the market is shifting to charcoal, which is easier to transport and more convenient to use in cramped urban quarters. However, widespread use of charcoal puts even greater stress on the environment because conversion from wood to charcoal requires twice as much timber to yield the same cooking energy.

In addition, once the conversion, transportation and combustion processes have been accounted for, charcoal emerges as one of the leading producers of carbon dioxide the most prevalent greenhouse gas. A meal cooked with charcoal produces three times more carbon dioxide than the same meal cooked with wood. On the other hand, charcoal can be made into a more efficient fuel by producing it in kilns that retain a higher proportion of the energy content within the charcoal. And the amount of charcoal used can be reduced by the use of more efficient charcoal stoves, which control airflow to the fuel and are insulated to minimize heat loss.

Looking for alternatives to fuelwood and its charcoal derivative, a number of communities are experimenting with solar box cookers and biogas digesters, both of which use renewable sources of energy and are pollutant-free and energy-efficient. The solar cookers and the digestors have been successful on a small and localised scale. The new methods have not been used on a big scale because of the high initial costs along with a variety of cultural biases and superstitions. For example, preparing and cooking food is an evening social activity, and solar cookers have to be used during the day. Biogas digestors are similarly constrained, since in some cultures the use of human and livestock waste, as fuel is unacceptable.

The fuelwood crisis is complicated one, and the easy, large-scale solutions that were originally recommended, such as the establishment of peri-urban plantations to increase wood fuel supplies, evidently will do little, if anything, to alleviate the problem. However, over the years, through mistakes and project failures, a few useful lessons have been learned. One such lesson—counter-intuitive though it may seem to many environmentalists—is that since biomas fuels will continue to play a major role for years to come, greater emphasis needs to be placed on finding ways to increase the woodfuel supply. Farmers, for example, can be encouraged to plant trees that will provide not only fuel but other products such as fruits, fodder, and lumber. And when the new high-efficiency stoves are made more widely available, the demand for trees will be reduced—even as their supply is increases.

33

Climate Change and Human Health

Changes in the India's climate, stemming from the greenhouse effect, are highly likely to damage human health. Food and fresh water supplies will be disrupted, millions of people displaced, and disease patterns altered dangerously and unpredictably.

Human health could be affected by even quite small changes in average mean temperature, and there is the prospect of some major diseases flourishing in warmer conditions and of more resistant strains of infection emerging.

The population in India most vulnerable to the negative impacts of global warming are in the lower-income groups, residents of coastal lowlands and islands, those living in semi-arid lands, and the urban poor in the squatter settlements, slums and shanty-towns of large cities.

Present strategies for immunisation, coping with disease vectors or carriers, providing safe drinking water, and improving nutrition are all based on existing climate regimes, ecosystems, and sea and solar radiation levels. These are all expected to change, but exactly how much cannot be predicted. It is therefore, virtually impossible to adjust health and nutritional strategies to take account of possible climate changes.

Humans can adapt to moderate changes in temperature and to occasional extremes. But this adaptive capacity is relatively low in infants and the elderly; it rises through childhood and adolescence to reach a maximum which can be maintained up to about 30 years of age.

A changing climate would alter the ecosystems of the vectors or agents which carry or cause many diseases, whether these be viruses, bacteria, parasites, plants, insects or other animals such as mosquitoes and snails. As the weather warms, the boundaries of the tropics may extend into the present subtropics, and parts of temperate areas may become subtropical. As air temperatures increase, some diseases will become common in regions which once rarely knew them and where there is little natural resistance to them. As result, death rates may also climb significantly.

It is possible that warmer weather around the world will cause increases in summer diseases and decreases in those associated with winter. Diseases contracted from both water and air will also spread more readily as ambient temperatures rise. In a warmer climate, mosquitoes and other vectors also may migrate vertically, up into highlands which were once too cold for them. This may be particularly hazardous in tropical highland areas where there is no natural resistance to malaiara.

Changes in temperature, rainfall, humidity and storm patterns may affect diseases borne by vectors in two ways. First, they will directly affect the vector's reproduction rate, biting rate, and the duration and frequency of human exposure. Second, they may modify agricultural systems or plant species, thus changing the relationship between host and vector. Development rates of malarial mosquitoes, for example, increase with warmer temperatures, but these pests need wet areas in which to breed.

Sea-level rise could also spread infectious disease by flooding sewerage and sanitation systems in coastal cities, and increase the incidence of diarrhoea in children. The flooding of hazardous waste dumps and sanitation systems could lead to long-term contamination of crop lands.

Rising seas may also disrupt marine habitats land aquatic food chains. Since fish constitute 40 per cent of all animal protein consumed by the people of India such a disruption of the marine ecosystem would affect the food supplies of many millions of people and dramatically increase protein deficiency and malnutrition. Changes in the availability of food and water, as well as radical shifts in disease patterns, could initiate large migrations of people, exacerbating food shortages, overcrowding, social stress and instability.

Some of the factors contributing significantly to global warming, such as the burning of fossil fuels and the use of chlorofluorocarbons (CFCs) and halons, threaten human health in other ways too. A typical petrol-driven motor car, for example, emits carbon monoxide, sulphur and nitrogen oxides, hydrocarbons, low-level ozone and lead-all of which are hazardous to health.

The ozone-depleting CFCs and halons pose a particular threat to humans through an increased risk of skin cancer, cataracts and lower immunity to other illnesses as a result of increased exposure to ultraviolet B radiation from the sun. Skin cancer risks are expected to rise most among fair-skinned.

34

Overcoming the Poverty in India and the Lessons Learned

Basic elements in the struggle against poverty in India are the provision of the economic services and assets which the poor have tended not to receive in the past—as a result of oversight or design. The emphasis on economic services and assets is just because the mass of the rural poor are self-employed, and it is upon the improvement in the means of production directly accessible to them that their prosperity depends. Health and education are very important, but offer more if combined with the material means of making a living—of putting body and mind to work. These assets and services include land, water, technology, commercial services, handling output and inputs, and credit—provided within an economic policy famework conductive to their optimal exploitation.

This list is hardly new. It corresponds to the requirements of any producer. The basic points to be made in this regard are: firstly, that the general requirements of poor producers are precisely the same as those of other producers and that measures to alleviate poverty that fall short of recognising the full range of such requirements are doomed to failure; and, secondly, that these assets and services are not typically provided in a form accessible to the poor. India has made important progress in providing a more effective framework for agricultural production "in general", this framework has not properly embraced small and poor producers. They are as follows:

Access to Land and Water

In the case of access to land, for example, land reform efforts in India has frequently involved major loop-holes, allowing the socially powerful to minimize *de facto* improvements in the condition of the poor. In the critical area of land rights, registration processes have been so complex and costly relative to the resources of the poor that land regularisation programmes have, sometimes unintentionally, become virtual characters for legalising the eviction of the poor and the actual loss of their traditional rights. Irrigation without specific measures to defend the interests of existing occupants of areas exposes them to expulsion—and, moreover, has tended to be concentrated in large-scale schemes benefiting already high potential areas in which the better-off predominate. While huge sums have been spent on large-scale irrigation schemes, little has been spent on water conservation and the sort of small-scale developments that are more likely to be of relevance to marginal small-scale producers.

Technology Transfer

In the area of technology, attention has been focused on technologies (such as the Green Revolution) requiring extensive access to water and fertilisers, neither of which are generally available among the poor. In fact, research almost every-where has concentrated on larger-scale production in areas of relatively high resource endowment. In contrast to this, research relevant to small-scale producers in marginal soil and rainfed areas in India has been shockingly deficient. As in other fields, this is partly explicable in terms of a frequently unproved belief that large-scale production is more efficient. It is also explicable in terms of the fact that it is the powerful who set the research agenda, not the poor. Taking its inspiration from highly specialised, large-scale agricultural units of production, research has tended to dwell separately on individual crops—rather than on the interaction between crops, which is of much greater relevance to small-scale producers engaging in highly complex systems of production to maximize food self-sufficiency and minimize risks.

Commercial Services

In the area of handling of output and inputs, organised services (not infrequently under public control in the past) have tended to concentrate in the proximity of large-scale producers and users of input in relatively well-endowed areas. In India the poor have had to incur the extraordinary costs of handling their own transport of goods to and from service points—frequently over long and deficient lines of communication. The alternative has been to resort to private intermediaries offering goods, and buying products, at prices very different from those enjoyed by larger producers. In effect, the better-off and the poor have confronted different sets of prices—with the poor paying more for what they buy, and receiving less for what they sell.

Credit

In the area of credit, the situation has been disastrous. It is generally recognised that productive improvement needs a change in means of production—new tools, improved seeds, fertilisers, etc. Such a change everywhere is typically effected on the basis of credit. Yet rural credit schemes in India have usually not extended support to small farmers and the poor. Credit has been concentrated among richer farmers with collateral and with demand for larger loans. In order to improve their productivity, the poor have been forced to seek credit from informal money-lenders—at virtually confiscatory rates. Again, the cost of modernisation has been much higher for the poor than for the better-off. The inevitable result has been a lower rate of change—and the consolidation, rather than the reduction of poverty.

The Victims Blamed

Although vast amounts of money have been invested in rural development in India, very little of it has reached the poor. The poor have been left to their own devices, while the better-off have received a wide range of assistance—not infrequently allowing them to encroach further upon the land of the poor. Support for agricultural expansion has not led to rural development, and it has not eliminated rural poverty. The relatively undynamic performance of many small-scale farmers under these circumstances is frequently taken as "proof" that they are a poor investment. This is a variant of "blaming the victim". In fact, the poor have fared badly, not because they could not efficiently use support, but because they did not get it.

In other words, the failure of the poor to benefit from agricultural sector investments has not reflected an economic failure among the poor themselves. Rather, it has involved policy and institutional failures. On the policy level, it has tended to reflect an unwillingness to restrain the socially influential from seeking to monopolise scarce resources to their own benefit—and, perhaps, a lack of awareness of the incompatibility between apparently "natural" criteria for support (e.g., the demand for land title as collateral for credit) and the particular circumstances of poor and small farmers (e.g., involvement in traditional forms of land tenure). On the institutional level, it has involved both unwillingness to give weight to the requirements of the poor, and lack of initiative in solving real problems in providing services to the poor such as the high cost of providing services on an individual basis to a large number of small and often dispersed "clients". While there has been a great deal of lamentation about poverty in India, remarkably little has been done to change it at the level of economic systems—perhaps because social welfare activities are much easier to implement than real policy and institutional changes. It is possible to do very much better—not by simply pouring in more resources (in channels which at times do not even ultimately reach the poor), but by changing the framework of investment, i.e., the instruments of development.

LESSONS LEARNED

Targeting of Resources

The fundamental lessons learned are that investment resources must be targeted at the poor. In a world of competition for scarce resources, investments in rural development tend to be captured by those with national and local power—a group, which rarely encompasses the rural poor. The first step in delivering resources to the poor is establishing strict criteria for eligibility for assistance. Indicators of wealth in India vary according to the nature of the local economy—in some cases it is extent of land ownership, in others size of cattle herds, in yet others ownership of draught animals—but the principle remains the same: investment in those with the least assets. In some cases, for example, where women represent a significant proportion of actual producers, this may give rise to entirely new patterns of investment.

Reorienting Institutions

The intention to distribute resources to the poorest is not always accompanied by actual performance. Among the reasons for this is the inappropriateness of delivery mechanisms. Put simply, institutions long oriented to the non-poor have tended to develop operating procedures and structures which reflect the nature of their de facto clientele and which hinder them from serving a new target group. In the area of credit, for example, insistence upon collateral in land may be an absolute obstacle to participation by the poor—just as a limited banking network may represent an obstacle to delivery to the poor, for whom the costs of communicating with a bank at considerable distance might well add significantly to the real cost of credit. Effectively channeling resources to the poor, therefore, means the elaboration of institutional means of delivery consistent with their circumstances.

However, it must be recognised that there are exceptional institutional costs associated with providing services to (and among) the poor—costs arising from the fact that there are many individuals involved, and that their individual requirement tend to be quite small. The costs of government services in, for example, agricultural credit, are necessarily higher if this involves a very large number of small producers than if it involves a small number of large producers. Administration costs in banking tend to be much higher relative to loan volume if it involves a myriad of individual small loans. These factors have often been adduced as reasons for the "impossibility" of serving the poor. Effective Service appears financially impossible, especially the context of widespread retrenchment in public expenditure under structural adjustment programmes. The poor are often willing to pay the actual costs of services—especially if the alternative is no service at all, or supply by local informal monopolists. On the other hand, there are proven ways of reducing costs of service supply to the poor—by involving the poor themselves. Everywhere in India poor people overcome some of the obstacles involved in their individual poverty through cooperation and joint action. While such organisation typically develops in the absence of formal service organisations and markets, it can also develop in association with formal organisations. In effect, the organised small farmer can help shoulder the cost of services through organising local level distribution and administration themselves.

People's Participation

People's participation is, therefore, not only a "social" concept. It is an eminently economic concept, involving cost sharing. It is fundamental to the sustainability of improvements. The long-term solution is not to throw money at the problems of the poor, but to help them to organize to overcome themselves. One of the happy externalities of this approach is not only lower cost services, but services more likely to be in harmony with what small farmers perceive themselves as needing.

Balanced Development

Development means change, not only in the volume of production, but in the composition of output and the conditions under which it is produced. What is argued is that the pursuit of development without the inclusion of the mass of small-scale producers and the poor has important structural drawbacks, and that their inclusion offers the basis for more sustainable long-term development. Some smallholder groups have a vast unutilised potential for expansion. Others have much more modest prospects.

Even those with the poorest assets and possibilities however, can be helped to improve their condition. While the direct economic benefits of this may be relatively slender, the side-effects may be great. An eventual shift of these groups to other areas and systems of production might be inevitable if aspirations for a better life are to be satisfied, but it is essential that this shift be orderly necessitating that support be given in the transitional period. This support can be either a direct welfare transfer or an investment in productive capacity. In many cases the latter may be the least-cost alternative.

The issue, then, is neither the "rich way" nor the "poor way". What is required is: an unprejudiced evaluation of the capacities and possibilities of poor and small-scale producers, and their potential role in the overall scheme of national development; allocation of investment resources according to potential and within an institutional framework ensuring delivery and profitable use; and a more balanced view of the overall social costs and benefits of alternative means of addressing transitional states. The belief is that the outcome of this will involve a reappraisal of the role of the poor in economic development, and a major improvement in the state of the rural poor throughout India.

The poor are many, their productive potential is great, but in few places is the exploitation of this potential an explicit focus of policy concern and action—although everywhere it is the concern of the poor themselves. While concrete evidence of the efficacy of systematic policy of support to the poor is sparse (simply because it has so rarely been tried), the evidence of its effectiveness on the local level is abundant.

35

Food Production

During the last 25 years, world agriculture successfully expanded food production faster than population growth. This can continue for the next 25 years and beyond, if appropriate action is taken. Although world food stocks are currently low and grain prices high, the world is not about to run out of food. We can produce enough food for future generation if we choose to do so.

The widespread food insecurity, unhealthy living conditions, and abject and absolute poverty in many developing countries are already threatening global stability. Failure to assure sustainable food security will foster the very conditions that will further destabilise and polarize the world in the years to come with tremendous consequences for all people.

The Basic Facts

Poverty is widespread in developing countries, with over 1.1 billion people living on a dollar a day or less per person. Human resource development in developing countries is lagging: 1 billion people lack access to health services, 1.3 billion do not have access to adequate sanitation systems, and one-third of primary school enrolls drop out by Grade 4. Natural resources, upon which future food production depends, are being degraded at alarming rates: almost 2 billion hectares of land have been degraded in the past 50 years: about 180 million hectares of forests have been converted to other uses during the 1980s, marine fisheries are collapsing around the world, and regional and seasonal water shortage afflict many developing countries. Improved appropriate technology is essential to increase productivity. Yet low-income food deficit developing countries are grossly under investing in agricultural research and many are reducing their support.

It calls for sustained action six priority areas. First, we must selectively strengthen the capacity of developing country governments to perform appropriate functions such as establishing or clarifying property rights, promoting private-sector competition in agricultural markets, and maintaining appropriate macro economic environments. Predictability, transparency and continuity in policy making and enforcement must be pursued.

Investing in People

Second, we must invest more in poor people in order to enhance their productivity, health, and nutrition. It is not only unethical but economically wasteful that a large share of the World's population is malnourished, illiterate, sick, and without access to productive resources. Access to primary education, primary health care, reproductive care and family planning information, and clean water and sanitation must be assured for all people. Access by the poor to productive resources and remunerative employment must be improved. Empowerment of women must be supported.

Third, we must accelerate agricultural productivity. Agriculture is the lifeblood of the economy in low-income developing countries. In those countries, it provides up to three-quarters of all employment and half of all incomes. There are very strong links between agricultural productivity increases and broad-based economic growth in the rest of the economy. Agriculture is an engine of growth in low-income developing countries. National and international agricultural research systems must be mobilised to develop improved technologies focused on developing countries, and extension systems must be strengthened to disseminate the improved technologies and techniques. Low-income countries currently spend less than 0.5 per cent of the value of agricultural production on agricultural research compared to 2 per cent spent on agricultural research in middle and high-income countries. An increase of agricultural research expenditures in low-income countries to at least 1 per cent of the value of agricultural output is urgently needed, with a longer term target of 2 per cent. National agricultural research must be supported by a vibrant international agricultural research system that undertakes research with large international benefits applicable across boundaries. Current investments in international agricultural research are grossly inadequate to provide the support needed by developing countries. It is of critical importance that agricultural research result in reduced unit costs of production. Such cost reductions will make food economically accessible to low-income consumers, and permit producer incomes to increase. To assure relevance of research and appropriate distribution of responsibilities, interactions between public sector agricultural research systems, farmers, private enterprises, and NGOs must be strengthened.

Fourth, we must assure sustainability in agricultural production and sound management of natural resources. Farmers, local communities, and governments must be encouraged to establish and enforce systems of rights to use and manage natural resources, to improve the way water is allocated and used, to reverse land degradation where it has occurred, to reduce the use of chemical pesticides and promote integrated pest management programmes, and to implement integrated soil fertility programmes in areas with low soil fertility. Local control over natural resources must be strengthened and local capacity for organisation and management improved. Investments in less-favoured geographical areas, that is, areas with agricultural potential, irregular rainfall patterns, and fragile soils must be expanded. Most poor people in developing countries reside in rural areas, and most rural poor reside in less-favoured areas. Yet, most investments, including agricultural research investments, still focus on the more-favoured areas. If we are serious about reducing poverty and protecting the natural resource base, the balance between the less-favoured and more-favoured areas must be redressed.

Fifth, we must reduce food-marketing costs in low-income developing countries. The cost of bringing food from the producer to the consumer is very high in many of these countries. Efficient, effective, and low-cost agricultural markets must be developed in order to bring these costs down. Inefficient state-run firms in agricultural in-put markets must be phased out; investment in developing and maintaining infrastructure, especially in rural areas, must be forthcoming; policies and institutions that favour large-scale, capital-intensive market agents over small-scale, labour-intensive ones must be removed; development of small-scale credit and savings institutions must be facilitated, and technical assistance to create or strengthen small-scale, labour-intensive competitive rural enterprises must be provided.

Sixth, we must expand and realign international development assistance. Many years ago, industrialised countries had agreed to allocate at least 0.7 per cent of the gross national product (GNP) to international assistance. Most countries have not reached or do not maintain this target. Not only must the industrialised countries increase international development assistance to reach the 0.7 per cent target, but they must realign it to low-income developing countries. Also contrary to the middle-and higher-income developing countries, the poorest countries are not able to gain access to capital from the rapidly expanding international commercial capital market. Developing countries in turn must seek measures to diversify sources of external funding, stem capital flight; and improve the effectiveness of the aid they receive.

36

Food Security

Availability and Access to Food

The world food situation has never been better. Enough food is being produced today that, if it were evenly distributed, no one should have to go hungry. World food production is increasing faster than population growth: per capita production increased by 5 per cent during the 1980s. Real food prices are at historic lows and have been declining for some time now. Yields of major cereals have more than doubled in the past three decades. These trends have contributed to complacency in some quarters regarding the world food situation.

Yet, more than 700 million people in the developing world do not have access to sufficient food to lead healthy and productive lives. More than 180 million children are underweight. Diseases of hunger and malnutrition are widespread. The desire to satisfy food needs has, in combination with increasing population densities and inadequate agricultural intensification, led to much degradation of environmentally fragile lands, such as forests and steep hillsides.

Over the next 20-30 years, farmers and policy makers in developing countries will be challenged to provide food at affordable prices for almost 100 million more people every year—the largest annual population increase in history. Moreover, they will have to increase food production from more productive use of the land and without further degradation of natural resources: area expansion is no longer a feasible option in most of the world.

What future food security will look like depends not on exogenous factors over which we have no control but on the decisions and actions taken by the major players: households, private and public sector agencies, governments, and the international community. If we continue to act as we have in the 1980s and early 1990s, more people will suffer from food insecurity it will be because some or all of these players failed to act in an appropriate and timely manner.

Feeding the World: Availability and Access to Food

There is enough food in the world today to feed everyone, if it were evenly distributed. Availability of daily food energy per capita in the developing countries as a whole increased by 0.7 per cent per year during the 1980s.

Twenty-five developing countries, including about half of the African countries, were unable to assure sufficient food energy (2,200 calories per person per day) for their populations at the end of the 1980s even if available food energy were evenly distributed within each country. This is down from 45 countries at the end of the 1970s.

However, available food is neither evenly distributed nor fully consumed. Availability of enough food at global, regional, or national levels does not necessarily mean that everyone is well fed. For people to be food secure—that is, to have access at all times to the food required for a healthy and productive life—there must be both availability of food and access to food. Access to food by households (and individuals) is conditioned by poverty: the poor usually lack adequate means to secure access to food.

Over 1.1 billion people in developing countries were living in poverty in 1993, more than 500 million in conditions of extreme poverty. South Asia is the home of about 50 per cent of the developing world's poor—more than 500 million people. Another 15 per cent are found in East Asia, 19 per cent in Sub-Saharan Africa, and 10 per cent in Latin America and the Caribbean. The prevalence of poverty (the proportion of each region's population that is poor) is very high—about 50 per cent—in South Asia as well as in Sub-Saharan Africa.

Today, there are more than 700 million people who do not have access to sufficient food to meet their needs for a healthy and productive life; they often go hungry, adults and children also suffer from diseases associated with hunger and poverty. For almost one fifth of the total population of developing countries to be chronically hungry tarnishes the images of a world that is now considered food-secure because it produces enough food.

Great progress has been made in meeting food needs during the last 30 years. For instance, the number of underfed people declined from an estimated 976 million in 1974-76 to 786 million in late 1980s. But the problem is far from solved. Keeping up with increasing needs and demands due to population growth, income increases, and dietary changes is itself a formidable challenge.

Hunger and food insecurity have a significant effect on health and nutrition of both adults and children. They can lead to growth failure in children. About 184 million pre-school children in developing countries were underweight in 1994. About 55 per cent of these underweight children were found in South Asia and another 16 per cent in Sub-Saharan Africa. The proportion of children that are underweight is higher in South Asia (almost 60 per cent), but it is also significant in Sub-Saharan Africa (30 per cent) and Southeast Asia (31 per cent). It is worrisome that the number of underweight children in Sub-Saharan Africa during the 1980s from 20 million to 28 million is particularly striking.

In addition to energy deficiencies, micro· nutrient deficiencies are also widespread in the developing world. About 14 million pre-school children (under the age of five years) have eye damage as a result of Vitamin-A deficiency.

Ten million of these children are found in Southeast Asia. Between 250,000 and 500,000 pre-school children go blind each year due to Vitamin-A deficiency, two-thirds of these children die within months of going blind. Many more children are mildly affected. Recently research has shown that even mild deficiencies can increase mortality significantly. Vitamin-A deficiencies are closely linked to diet, which can be influenced by agricultural research and policy.

Iron deficiency affects about 1 billion people in the world, particularly children and women of reproductive age. Iron deficiency leads to anaemia, which if not checked can diminish learning capacity and increase morbidity and morality. In the developing countries, about 370 million women between 15 and 49 years of age—42 per cent of this population group—where anaemic in the 1980s. Almost one-half were in South Asia. And there are tentative indications from South Asia and Sub-Saharan Africa that the prevalence of anaemia is rising in non pregnant adult women of reproductive ages.

In Sub-Saharan Africa, this trend is undoubtedly associated with deterioration in general standards of living, including increased poverty and food insecurity. Anaemia partly arises from diets insufficient in iron, which again could be addressed through agricultural research and policy. For example, a possible reason why iron deficiency and anaemia are going up in South Asia may lie in the decrease in production of iron rich pulses during that same period, which in part reflects the larger research input into competing crops such as wheat in South Asia. This emphasizes the importance of considering the effects on diet and thus on health and nutrition in setting research priorities for yield-increasing research.

South Asia is the home of about half of the developing world's hungry and food-insecure people, but this population group is growing rapidly in Sub-Saharan Africa. Much of the poverty and food insecurity is in rural areas, mainly in low-potential areas such as arid zones, but urban poverty is also growing rapidly.

Four Key Factors will Influence Future Food Production and Consumption

Global and regional food production and consumption during the next 10-20 years will be influenced by a large number of factors. Changes in the following four sets of factors are likely to particularly important:

1. Economic growth and economic policies;
2. Population growth and urbanisation;
3. Rural infrastructure, agricultural production technology, and access to modern inputs; and
4. Natural resource management and environmental consideration.

The expected impact of each of these factors on future food production and consumption is considerable.

Economic Growth and Economic Policies

Economic growth must resume in the developing world, especially in Sub-Saharan Africa. To support such growth, it is critical to:

- complete structural adjustment and economic reforms;
- remove external barriers to growth such as trade distortions and subsidies in developed countries;
- liberalise trade and remove market distortions;
- enhance access by the poor to land, capital, and technology;
- expand investment in rural infrastructure, health, education, and agricultural research and technology;
- facilitate sustain ability in agricultural production; and
- reverse the decline in international assistance to agriculture.

Growth in real per capita income during the 1980s was disappointing for developing countries as a whole. However, the low average rate of growth covers large variations among regions. The high rates of economic growth in Asia are expected to continue through the 1990s, while incomes in Sub-Saharan Africa are expected to keep pace with population growth.

Future economic growth depends on internal policies as well as on the international policies as well as on the international environment. The extent to which current structural adjustment and economic reforms in Latin America, Sub-Saharan Africa, the Commonwealth of Independent States (CIS), Eastern Europe, and selected countries in Asia and the Middle East are carried to successful completion at an appropriate speed and sequence is of paramount importance for future economic growth in those countries.

Closely related to this issue is the question of the most appropriate role of the state in a market-oriented economy with inappropriate institutions, poor infrastructure, and insufficient experience by the private sector in dealing effectively in a competitive market environment. Overreaction to past failures such as excessive and inappropriate state intervention may cause governments to take on a passive role where intervention is needed to assure that the markets function effectively and to deal with outside influences on the economy.

Future economic growth will also depend on the international trade environment, including trade distortions by developed countries, and access to external aid. Import restrictions for agricultural and non-agricultural products in Japan, the European Union, and the United States, along with domestic agricultural subsidies and implicit and explicit export subsidies for agricultural products, are of particular concern.

Population Growth and Urbanisation

If progress in economic growth is not to be undermined by rapid population growth and excessive urbanisation, effective population and migration policies are necessary to complement growth-oriented policies. Such policies must focus on:

- universal access to family planning information and technology; and
- incentives to reduce rural-urban migration, such as provision of employment in rural areas and stimulation of agricultural and non-agricultural growth in rural areas.

Although the annual growth rate is falling for the world as a whole, the population increase during the next 20-30 years, of slightly less than 100 million people a year, will be the largest ever. Approximately 97 per cent of this increase is projected to occur in the Third World, with Africa alone accounting for 34 per cent of the growth. Thus although reductions in annual population growth rates have begun to occur in Asia and Latin America, they are insufficient to counter the absolute increases. Population growth rates of these magnitudes will greatly increase the need for food and other basic necessities.

Rural Infrastructure, Agricultural Production Technology, and Access to Modern Inputs

Continued progress in all three of these areas is critical to future food security.

- Resources must be committed to infrastructure construction and maintenance. Labour-intensive public works programmes are a viable mechanism for building roads, reforesting areas, and engaging in soil conservation projects, while creating employment and income in rural areas.
- International and national agricultural research must continue to develop yield-enhancing production technology, especially in maize, millet, and other crops, as well as build tolerance or resistance in crops to pests and adverse climatic conditions.

- Farmer access to modern inputs must be facilitated through provision of credit and technical assistance. Inputs must be made available to all farmers on time and in required amounts.

The importance of investments in rural infrastructure within the context of rapid urbanisation has already been established. Even without rapid urban growth, however, such investments are needed in many developing countries, particularly the poorest ones, to facilitate agricultural and rural development. Improved rural infrastructure enhances access to export markets, modern production inputs, and consumer goods. It reduces marketing costs, promotes exchange between intracountry markets, reduces spatial and temporal price distortions, and, in general, increases efficiency in production and marketing.

However, while essential, effective rural infrastructure alone is not enough to assure agricultural and rural development and rapid increases in food production in developing countries. Yield enhancing production technology is of critical importance. Although opportunities for expansion of agricultural production into lands not currently under cultivation still exist in some countries, such opportunities are so limited that they would probably not be able to counter losses of current agricultural lands to alternative uses on a global level. Furthermore, attempts to expand agricultural production into new lands would, in most cases, require large investments in technology, tools and materials and would increase the risk of land degradation and deforestation. Thus, future increases in food production must come primarily from higher yields per unit of land rather than from land expansion.

Agricultural research has successfully developed yield-enhancing technology for the majority of crops grown in temperate zones and for several crops grown in tropical zones. The dramatic impact of agricultural research and modern technology on wheat and rice yields in Asia and Latin American since the mid-1980s is well known. Less dramatic but significant yield gains have been obtained from research and technological change in other crops, particularly maize.

Natural Resource Management and Environmental Considerations

Research, technology development, incentives, and regulations are needed to prevent environmental degradation. These measures include appropriate water management policies, reduction of subsidies that encourage wasteful use of inputs better definition of ownership and user rights to resources including land, education of farmers to encourage appropriate use of technology and resource conservation, and the provision of alternatives to resource-degrading inputs and techniques. Since poverty is a major source of degradation, poverty eradication is justified also on environmental grounds.

The recent surge in public and private concerns about negative environmental effects of economic growth and development may, if sustained, have important implications for agricultural development and future food production and consumption. Of particular concern of the need to avoid degradation of natural resources such as land and water, as well as deforestation, water contamination, and health risks associated with the use of chemicals. Since most of the current and potential resource degradation and environmental contamination result from situations in which those who cause and possibly benefit from degradation do not pay the costs, neither the market nor the individual producers and consumers are likely to incorporate preventive measures into their behaviour. Only when sufficient damage has been done to influence significantly current or future production costs will market and producer behaviour change. The state is more likely to undertake preventive measures either through publicly funded research and technology development or through incentive policies and regulations. Extensive water logging, salination, and associated land degradation and productivity losses resulting from inappropriate water management are of particular concern in large parts of Asia.

No Time for Complacency

Population growth will outstrip growth in food production in Sub-Saharan Africa for a long time to come unless more is done to accelerate agricultural growth. Between now and 2000, the population will grow at more than 3 per cent a year, while food production is likely to grow at 2 per cent or less a year. By the year 2000, the production shortfall is estimated to increase to about 50 million tons of grain equivalent, up from the current level of about 14 million tons. The region will not have the necessary foreign exchange to import such large amounts of food. And African governments will not be able to count on enough food aid to make up the difference. If current trends continue, by the year 2020, Africa will have a food shortage of 250 million tons, which is more than 20 times the current food gap.

Poverty is expected to increase rapidly in the coming years. Sub-Saharan Africa's share of the world's poor is expected to increase from the current 19 per cent to about 28 per cent in 2000. Furthermore, the number of underweight children is expected to increase in the 1990's in Sub-Saharan Africa.

Asian demand for cereals is estimated to grow at an annual rate of 2.1 per cent between now and the year 2000, where as food production is expected to grow at 1.9 per cent per year. Much of the production shortfall is likely to be dealt with through expanded imports and perhaps through expanded regional production in response to price increases.

In Latin America, by contrast, growth in food production is anticipated to exceed food demand growth: food production is estimated to grow by 3 per cent annually between 1990 and 2000, while food demand is estimated to grow by 2.5 per cent per year.

Large areas of land are rapidly being degraded and deforested. And the principal reasons for environmental degradation—poverty, high population growth, and limited access to appropriate agricultural technology—are not being dealt with effectively.

About 700 million people are food insecure for them the food crisis has arrived. For the 10-12 million preschool children who died in 1994 from hunger and diseases related to malnutrition, the food crisis came and went. One-third of the preschool children of the Third World are unable to grow to their full potential and face increased risk of death and disease.

Complacency is not in order. Clearly, Malthus underestimated the power of science to expand food production. The mass starvation that was predicted for Asia in the 1970s and 1980s did not occur because science was effectively put to work to expand crop yields. However, past yield increases came about people with foresight made appropriate decisions. The failure to expand investments in agricultural research and technology development during the 1980s and 1990s indicates that such foresight no longer prevails. Given the long lag time between investment in agricultural research and the resulting production increases, failure to invest today will show up in production shortfalls 10 to 20 years from now. The problems associated with environmental degradation will present themselves sooner. We must not wait until a global food crisis is upon us or until the last tree has fallen to make these investments.

REFERENCES

1. FAO, FAO Production Yearbook.
2. FAO, "The State of Food and Agriculture 1992".
3. FAO, "Agriculture Towards 2010".
4. FAO, "The State of Food and Agriculture 1994".
5. FAO, Food Outlook (December 1994).
6. World Bank, World Development Report 1995.

7. World Bank, Global Economic Prospects and the Developing Countries.

8. World Food Programme, Food Aid in Review (Rome WFP 1992).

9. World Bank, Global Economic Prospects and the Developing Countries 1992. (Washington, D.C.: World Bank).

Bibliography

Anand, R.P., *Legal Regime of Sea Bed and the Developing Countries,* 1975.

Bhatt, S., *Environment Protection and International Law,* Radiant Publication, Kalkaji, New Delhi, 1985, pp. 122.

Bhatt, S., *Environmental Laws and Water Resources Management,* Radiant Publication, India, and Advent Books Inc. New York, 1986, pp. 355.

Behrman, Danial, *In Partnership with Nature—UNESCO and the Environment* (Paris, 1973).

Bell, Daniel, "Technology, Nature and Society", *American Scholar,* Summer 1973.

Bentley, Glass, *"Biology and Human Values",* USIS, New Delhi.

Book of Nature. The Way Things Work, published by George Allen and Unwin Ltd., 1981, pp. 525.

Boulding, Kenneth E., "New Goals for Society", S.H. Schun, ed., *Energy, Economic Growth and the Environment.*

Carr, E.H., *What is History,* 1961.

Darlington, C.D., *The Evolution of Man and Society* (London, 1961).

Downing, Paul B., ed., *Air Pollution and Social Sciences* (New York, 1971).

"Drive to adopt national water policy", *Times of India,* 22 July, 1983.

Dubos, Rene, "Man and his Environment", *Britannica Perspectives,* Vol. 1, 1968.

Einstein, A., *My Views,* ed., by S.K. Bandopadhyaya (Calcutta, 1976).

"*Environment Research Programme*", prepared by NCEPC, Department of Science and Technology, New Delhi.

Forbes, R.J., "The Conquest of Nature and its Consequences", *Britannica Perspectives,* Vol. 1, 1968.

Fowler, John M., *Energy and Environment* (New York, 1975).

Fuller, Buckminister, R., *Operating Manual for Spaceship Earth* (New York, 1969).

Gandhi, Indira, "Poverty Greatest Pollution, says Mrs. Gandhi", *Times of India,* 8 September, 1981.

Glenn, Seaborg, "*Science, Technology and Development: A New World Outlook*", USIS, New Delhi.

Hacoley, Amos H., *Human Ecology* (New York, 1950).

India Must Develop Own Ecology", *Times of India,* 8 October 1981.

Marion, Jerry B., *Energy in Perspective* (London, 1974).

Misra, K.C., *Manual of Plant Ecology,* New Delhi, 1980.

Mukherji, P.K., *Life of Tagore,* trans, by S.K. Ghosh, 1975.

Mumford, Lewis, "The Future of Cities", in *Basic Issues in Environment,* E.J. Winn, ed., 1972.

Palmslierna, H., *Future Imperatives for Human Environment,* 1972.

Pavithran, A.K., "World Futurology", *Eastern Journal of International Law* (Madras), Vol. 9.

"Plans to Usher India into 21st Century", *Times of India,* 24 October, 1985.

Polunin, Nicholas, "The Biosphere Today", *The Environmental Future,* Proceedings of 1st International Conference on Environmental Future in Finland, ed. by N. Polunin, 1972.

Radhakrishnan, S., *Recovery of Faith,* 1967.

Report on the State of Environment Prepared by Centre for Science and Environment, New Delhi, 1985.

Sarkar, Mahendra Nath, *The Cultural Heritage of India*, Vol. 1.

Sen, Sudhir, "Blueprint for a Better World", *Times of India*, 2 March, 1980.

The Limits to Growth, A Report to Club of Rome (New York, 1972).

The Mind of J. Krishnamurti, ed. by L.S.R. Vas (Bombay, 1971).

Toynbee, Arnold, "Man and his Soul", *Hindustan Times*, 4 January, 1968.

United Nations List of National Parks and Protected Areas, 1985.

Vivekananda, Swami, *Complete Works*, Vol. II (Calcutta, 1968).

Ward, Barbara and Dubos Rene, *Only one Earth: The Care and Maintenance of a Small Planet*, Report to UN Conference on Human Environment, Stockholm, 1972.

"Wildlife Laws in India", *Times of India*, 4 March, 1985.

Ward, Barbara, *Progress for a Small Planet*, 1979.

INDEX